Giving Your Child
the Excellence Edge

FOCUS ON THE FAMILY®

Giving Your Child the Excellence Edge

10 Traits Your Child Needs to Achieve Lifelong Success

Vicki Caruana

TYNDALE

Tyndale House Publishers, Wheaton, Illinois

A Focus on the Family book published by
Tyndale House Publishers, Wheaton, Illinois

Focus on the Family books are available at special quantity discounts when purchased in bulk by corporations, organizations, churches, or groups. Special imprints, messages, and excerpts can be produced to meet your needs. For more information, contact: Focus on the Family Sales Department, 8605 Explorer Drive, Colorado Springs, CO 80920; or phone (800) 932-9123.

Library of Congress Cataloging-in-Publication Data

Caruana, Vicki.
  Giving your child the excellence edge : 10 traits to help your child achieve lifelong success / Vicki Caruana.
      p. cm.
At head of title: Focus on the family.
  ISBN 1-58997-131-0
  1. Education—Parent participation. 2. Academic achievement. I. Title.
LB1048.5.C38 2004
371.19'2—dc22

                                                              2003019678

Editor: Mick Silva
Cover Design: Amy Kiechlin
Photos: Mark Waters
Cover Copy: Joy Olson
Text Design: Angela Barnes

Printed in the United States of America
1 2 3 4 5 6 7 8 9 / 09 08 07 06 05 04

To my husband, Chip, and my children, Christopher and Charles

I would also like to thank the wonderful people at Focus on the Family who joined with me to make this book possible.

Contents

Introduction

When I taught gifted education for Pinellas County Schools in Florida, I was impressed by the ideals behind the program. They used no standardized curriculum; teachers had the freedom to teach whatever allowed them to fulfill the requirements for student competency. Often as I was teaching, I would be struck with how the strategies I was trying to instill were ones that could easily benefit any student—no matter the level of "giftedness."

Then, in 1990, a report was generated in response to *Blueprint 2000,* the president's study of American education. Called the SCANS report, it outlined many areas every child needed to acquire competency to become successful, productive members of society.[1] As I began to incorporate these fundamental areas into my teaching program, I was again amazed to realize not only how easily *every* child could learn and benefit from them, but how *biblical* the basic building blocks of excellence really were.

Yet my greatest realization about the universal importance of these skills didn't occur until I began raising my own children and I started seeing these concepts changing our lives. It soon became my greatest passion to teach these biblically based concepts to as many children as possible. My mission has become to help parents make the necessary yet simple connections between a child's success at home, in school, and later out in the world. And because these concepts are based on universal truth, they apply to everyone whether parent or child, student or teacher, Catholic or Protestant, Jew or Gentile.

I am confident that *Giving Your Child the Excellence Edge* will help you take advantage of the intrinsic abilities your child already possesses.

As you walk through these chapters, I think you will realize as I did how revolutionary these simple principles truly are. My humble hope is that you will find the task of guiding your child toward excellence as spiritually rewarding for you as it has been for me.

Since each child will have certain strong and weak areas to focus on, I've designed the material to allow you to pick and choose the skills your child needs most. The activities and action points in each chapter are designed to make encouraging those little minds quick, easy, and enjoyable. A small daily activity is all that's required to give your child the greatest possible chance of achieving every goal he sets in life. As we'll discuss, you have been chosen, for better or worse, as your child's "Life Coach": you must model and practice these skills to encourage the seeds of excellence to grow. You'll also find that teaching these strategies gets easier with practice. I invite you to rediscover the ten skills in this book as the stepping-stones that lead you to successful, productive adulthood.

We *all* want to give our children an excellent life. Passing on these ten basic skills will make *all* the difference.

Chapter One

Your Child's Best Teacher Is You

"Listen, my son, to your father's instruction
and do not forsake your mother's teaching."
—PROVERBS 1:8

What did you learn in school today?"

"I don't know."

"Well, you must have learned something. What did you do: sit around all day and stare at one another?"

"I guess."

You stare at your son, your hands on your hips. His tired body is slumped down on the couch as he soaks in the cartoons. If you looked at it from his perspective, you might realize he's actually *trying* to shed all memory of the school day. All you're asking is for a few words to fill in the details, but to him your interrogation seems like something closer to torture.

On the other hand, what message are you sending your child if you never asked about his school day? Would you be telling him that his education was important to you or that you were interested in what he was learning?

Or would he think you cared as little for what he was learning as he did?

As a teacher, I watched some students agonize over a lower mark than their usual *A*, while others flippantly boasted about getting an *F*. I'd watch in wonder at what must have been going on in the underachieving children's homes. What behaviors and attitudes were they picking up from their parents?

It's a fact that your child learns most of his or her life lessons—including the one on the importance of education—from you. We all sense that this is true, but it is rare to see a parent who really knows it *and* acts on it.

Think about it for a moment: *What has your child learned from you today?*

If your answer is "Hmmm . . ." you're not alone! For most American parents, the thought of adding one more thing to their already-long list of chores is virtually unbearable. But while these strategies can help you provide the very best education for your child, without a daily investment of time, attention, and effort on your part, your child will never pick them up. You must dedicate the time. This book can be a helpful resource when a particular need arises, but ideally you will apply these strategies on a daily basis and begin to see immediate benefits from your investment. As in the area of finances, even a minor investment of time can reap huge dividends when it's properly placed. And while there is no "quick fix," these tools will help you point your child toward his personal and educational goals.

Helping your child put these strategies to use will foster his long-term success. The only prerequisites are your willingness to try and your ability to keep an open mind.

But I'm Not a Teacher!

Many parents feel inadequate when considering their responsibility to teach their children. Yet educators all speak of the fact that nothing they teach children in a classroom has nearly the effect of a parent's teaching in the home. If you are a parent, you are a teacher. Think of all the things you've already taught your child: the intricacies of every family, your values and beliefs, what to do or not to do in a given situation. You communicated so many "firsts" to your child—whether you realize it or not. We teach our children both the positive *and* the negative things about life: whom to trust and whom to hate, how to share and how to get your own way, how to help others and how to hurt them. Certainly, other people also contribute to our children's development. But as parents, we are the primary teachers of what this business of living is all about.

Your decision to think about *what* you say and do each day makes it easy to see *why* your children say and do what they do each day.

Setting Your Sights

Before we rush into making "achievers" out of our children, it's important to first consider our goals. These 10 skills will be powerful tools for pointing your child toward the bull's-eye—the fulfillment of goals in her life. Yet if your "bull's-eye" doesn't match hers, you may be in for a bit of a struggle.

Your idea of success is probably different from your child's, at least right now. But rather than simply working to bring his idea of success in line with yours, ask yourself, *For whom am I really doing this, and why?* Government reports on education have simple enough goals: to develop a working system for creating productive members of society. Is that your goal, or is yours more personal, based on a deeper belief system? Do your children know your goals for them (or even their goals for themselves, for that matter)?

It is likely you will need to discuss this as a family and commit to agreeing on a few basic goals together before you start applying these tools. We'll discuss this further in chapter three.

Where Should My Child Go to School?

Another obvious but important consideration is what type of school your child should attend. The debate surrounding school choice rages on. My purpose is not to tell you which is best for your child. But to set your children up to succeed in life, finding the proper school for them is very important. If your child is not thriving in his current environment, you may need to consider a more suitable choice. Whether it's a public or private school, a charter or magnet school, or even homeschooling, your choices are critical to their development.

Actually, the fact that parents even *have* a choice is largely a new phenomenon. Over recent decades, more and more options have become available, such as more affordable private schools and the emergence of charter and magnet schools. Of course, having this many choices makes it important to check into each option thoroughly before making a decision. In the end, remember that the decision is never set in stone. You can always reconsider if it isn't working for your child.

Consider some basic advantages and disadvantages of the different schooling options:

Public Schools

Public education offers traditional schooling at its best—*and* its worst. Yet for many families, this remains the best choice. The quality of any public school depends primarily upon three factors: the dedication of the teachers, the involvement of the parents, and the availability of funds. The first two carry the most weight. Even with a shortage of funds students can excel. Many inner city or small rural schools prove this. By the same token, there are some schools in very wealthy districts that are producing mediocre test scores. As we know, the battle is won in the classroom, one student at a time.

Do you or your child remember a favorite teacher? What was special about him or her? Did he have an uncommon concern for students? Would you say she loved her job? How was the communication with parents—was it regular or infrequent? Was the teacher innovative, teaching in a way that was encouraging and inspiring? Did he take the time to get to know the children well?

Obviously, it doesn't take private funding for schools to offer a good education. When teachers find fulfillment in their job, it makes up for many other things a school might lack.

Advantages

1. Public schools are good at reaching and helping the below-average student.
2. Public schools are driven by common standards and goals.
3. Public schools are free.
4. Public schools offer students a variety of social experiences based upon diverse populations.

Disadvantages

1. Public schools are overcrowded.
2. Public schools often lack funds.
3. Public schools do not effectively address the needs of gifted students. They are set up to care for the needs of the below-average student and increasingly the average student. Minimum standards are in place.
4. Public schools have more student safety concerns than the others.
5. Public schools can be more "forward-thinking" than many parents might prefer.

6. As is common in politics, "reform" can often mean a previously failed approach repackaged under a new name.

Private Schools

Private schooling is the oldest form of institutionalized education in the United States. When our nation was formed, formal schooling was privatized: It was only for older children (12 to 14 years old), whose parents could afford both the tuition and the shortage of that child's work on the farm. Today, private schools are available to a wider range of students, but they still carry the high price tag. Scholarships are usually available on a limited basis. For the most part, private schools do a good job of stretching funds to attract less affluent parents who have become dissatisfied with poor public school programs.

Even so, private schools are prone to special problems. Some schools will enroll students who have been asked to leave a public school for discipline reasons, effectively making them into a reformatory school for some. And recent salary boosts in public schools have wooed many good teachers away from struggling private institutions. Even with regular tuition increases, a private school teacher's salary often stays the same, which may account for the high rate of uncertified teachers in private schools. Still, private schooling is preferable for many reasons.

Advantages

1. Private schools are often church-affiliated and may support your desire to impart faith in your child's education.
2. Private schools typically have a higher level of parental involvement.
3. A community atmosphere can encourage greater solidarity and discipline among students.

4. Accelerated curricula for gifted students is usually offered.

5. Although some private schools can be overcrowded, they generally have a smaller class size.

Disadvantages

1. Although private schools must undergo an accreditation process, some schools (and teachers) have not earned accreditation.

2. Private schools that have earned accreditation will be more expensive.

3. Problem students sent from public schools may derail opportunities for creativity and classroom innovation.

4. Parents must often transport their own children to school.

5. If a private school is church-affiliated, it may support a denomination with differing doctrinal views from the parents.

Charter/Magnet Schools

Charter and magnet schools are public schools that are designed to meet an identified need in the community.

The newest of available schooling choices, charter schools are actually public schools that are funded by businesses or communities who want the highest level of involvement in their children's education; many are run more like a private school than a typical public school. A charter school, then, may not be run by educators or government, but by industries. While the teachers and administration usually choose the curriculum, the typical supporter is a wealthy parent. In many cases, a group of parents begins a charter school to target a specific population of children, whether it be gifted, at-risk, artistic, or low-income students.

Magnet schools are similar, but with one major difference: They too serve a specified population, but usually as a school-within-a-school

program. For example, International Baccalaureate programs (IB) may be offered at a public high school and students interact only with other students in the program. Many magnet schools exist entirely on their own funding. They almost always have a waiting list, and some have even begun deciding enrollment with a lottery system.

Advantages
1. Because they are publicly funded, there is no tuition cost.
2. They typically offer a smaller class size.
3. They may target a specific need of your child.
4. They allow for greater parental input.
5. Due to high parent involvement and visibility, they may have fewer disciplinary problems and safety concerns than both private and public schools.

Disadvantages
1. They may not be conveniently located, and the parent is usually responsible for transportation.
2. Waiting lists can be very long.
3. With such a high level of parental involvement, disagreements can sometimes disrupt programs.

Homeschooling
It is believed that homeschooled children make up approximately 3 percent of the school-age population.[1] Recent high profile studies have thrust homeschooling into the mainstream culture. The studies are showing that a homeschooling parent's love and dedication far outweigh their lack of certification. Not only is one-on-one attention better for children, the school day can be much more efficient, and therefore shorter,

opening up a myriad of other opportunities that are unavailable in other settings.

Home school is able to combine a variety of approaches to meet the individual needs of the child. And with the growing participation in homeschool co-ops, socialization is becoming greater and more diverse all the time.

Of course, as this choice grows in popularity, its proponents are splintering into factions of educational philosophies. The "unschoolers" utilize many different types of curriculum, while the traditionalists try to mimic a "school-at-home" approach as much as possible.

Homeschooling is not for every child. Nor is it the best choice for every family every year. It can be a difficult situation to "work where you sleep" for both parent and child. The sacrifices can be great. But its proponents say that the benefits of homeschooling outweigh the sacrifice on a daily basis.[2]

Advantages

1. Homeschooling best meets the individual learning needs of children.
2. Homeschooling can create or strengthen the family bond.
3. Parents can set their own schedule and choose their own curricula.
4. Prestigious colleges and universities seek out and welcome home-schooled students.

Disadvantages

1. Parental burnout can frequently occur in the absence of a strong support system.
2. The financial sacrifice of changing to a one-income family is too great for many.

3. The choice to homeschool is still criticized and questioned by many.

Get Involved!

You don't have to be your child's actual schoolteacher to be involved in his education. But it will take more than volunteering in a classroom one hour a week to have a real impact. Research shows that parental involvement in a child's education is directly linked to that child's success. Yet according to a recent study made by the U.S. Department of Education, 91 percent of teachers say that lack of parental involvement is still a problem.[3]

What parents must realize is that their involvement in their child's education is as important as any other area of their lives and requires as much attention. Just as we must be active, informed participants in health care today, we must also be active, informed advocates of our children's education. This doesn't happen if your level of involvement is to drop your child off at school and assume all is well until you pick her up each afternoon. To be *informed* you must get *involved*. Here are three primary ways to get involved in your child's education:

Become Aware

There are many things you can do to become aware of your child's educational experience. Get the school's perspective—not just your child's—on what is being taught. Read everything that comes home with your child, from their homework to the school newsletter. Check out the school's Web site. Attend PTA meetings. Join a school advisory committee, if one exists. Set up conferences with all your child's teachers *before* a problem crops up. Engage your child in conversation about school at a time when he is more likely to talk about it—at bedtime or in the car.

Make the effort! When you do, you'll never be able to say, "I didn't know," or "I wasn't aware."

Be Visible

Most parents come to school only for special events and then are never seen again. But you know you're involved when you walk into the front office and the secretary knows you by name! In order for that familiarity to take place, you must volunteer some of your time at the school. And when you do, volunteer somewhere other than your own child's classroom! Join the PTA and help to set up events or fundraisers. Thank those involved with your child in a tangible way. Food works wonders, especially sweets! If you're visible, when a problem arises, teachers and staff will be more likely to contact you right away. And if you're approachable, they won't hesitate to include you in the inside information.

Be Your Child's Advocate

The word *advocate* can mean so many things: a backer, a fighter, a follower, a patron, a proponent, a savior, a spokesman, or a sponsor. But each of these synonyms implies an active role. When you are someone's "advocate," you believe in them and their message to such an extent that you deliberately and actively promote their interests and protect their reputation. Our children are not capable of being their own advocates. It's up to us to *back* their pursuits, *fight* for their rights, *follow* their lead in how they learn, be their *patron* by supporting their talents, be a *proponent* for their needs, *save* them from dangerous situations, *speak* up on their behalf, and *sponsor* their efforts at achieving success. They, in turn, will learn to do the same for themselves and their children.

Remember that in every school, no matter which one you choose, there are things that will go wrong. It's the nature of life! Yet if you stay aware, make yourself visible, and become an advocate for your children, you will

have the necessary tools to address any problem that might arise. And from your efforts, your child will learn what living in this world requires.

Isn't that the real goal?

Choosing a Particular School

As time goes on, choosing a school is only getting harder. Gone are the days when you just enrolled in the neighborhood school with everyone else, no decisions to make, no responsibilities, no need to check things out. Today, it is important to remember that *more* choices don't always mean *better* choices. But how can we wade through the process without getting bogged down by the potential problems?

Before enrolling your child in any particular school, ask yourself the following questions:

- *What kind of person will this school encourage my child to become?*
- *What are the major academic, social, and emotional needs of my child? Will his various needs be met in this school's environment on a short-term basis? On a long-term basis?*
- *Will the atmosphere of this school cultivate or hinder his growth?*
- *How much input can I have as a parent in this school?*
- *What are my options if I disagree with the decisions made at this school?*
- *What level of involvement is needed by my child to succeed? Does this school support or encourage that level of involvement?*
- *What does this school expect from parents?*
- *What do I expect from the teachers in this school? Are my expectations reasonable?*

You may have to do some searching to find the answers, but it's worth the effort. What and how much our children learn is greatly dependent upon what we provide for them with our time and effort. It can be humbling to realize that the buck stops with you, but don't let the responsibility of the task intimidate you. Schools know the parents who are involved, and they listen to them.

So be encouraged! You're taking the first step toward giving your child the best education he can have.

Chapter Two

A Quality Producer

"So whether you eat or drink or whatever you do,
do it all for the glory of God."
—1 Corinthians 10:31

What is *quality*? The Temptations defined its main component in the title of their song "The Way You Do the Things You Do": It's often not *what* we do, but *how* we do it that matters. Quality is respected, often expected, and primarily responsible for customer satisfaction, or the lack thereof. In a nutshell, *quality* means doing more than was expected—above and beyond the call of duty. An early *commitment to quality* can have both immediate and future benefits for your child's development and later success in life. If our children are going to grow into adults of quality who produce quality work, we can help them by cultivating that ability when they are young. And school is one of the best training grounds in which to practice doing quality work.

Commit to Quality

The pursuit of quality emerges from a *commitment* to continuous improvement. In the beginning of—and throughout—your child's education, your goal should be to help your child look for ways to improve. But without an informed understanding of your commitment to quality it is easy to begin to accept what was previously unacceptable. A commitment to quality, then, like "quality control," ensures you are never settling for second best. Just as you desire quality from the products you buy, the people you are served by, and the performances you observe, your own commitment to quality will come from your desire to see your child's work defined by excellence.

Quality Products

How well something is produced is often a hot topic of discussion. Whether you felt a purchase was worth the money you paid or you felt the workmanship was shoddy, your desire to purchase quality products influences your buying decision. Similarly, quality work influences employers' decisions. These days, it is rare for an individual's name to actually go on their work, causing workers to lack a sense of pride in what is produced. Yet poor workmanship is poor regardless of whether or not it is signed by its creator, and employers—both current and future ones—will notice poor quality in the workplace.

Hiding behind unacceptable work does not lead to success. Our children must be encouraged to create the best product they can, as often as they can. They must be shown that school projects, even daily homework assignments, are opportunities to create quality products. They need to feel that they can stand behind their products proudly and say, "Here's my best! Take a look."

How we do what we do helps to define us, and builds our reputation. What kind of person does your child want to be known as? Is he someone who does the bare minimum to get by, or someone who goes the extra mile? When I was a teacher, I quickly learned the reputation of each student by the work he or she produced. I could tell by book reports and science projects who had an understanding of quality and who did not. Some of us didn't learn the value in doing a quality job until much later in life. Your children shouldn't have to wait to understand the importance of quality.

Quality Processes

The steps we take to create quality products are just as important as the products themselves. If the process we use or the manner in which we create them is flawed, then the product will be flawed as well. The student who waits until the night before his end-of-the-semester project is due to even begin, is not only putting stress on the entire family, but is undermining the end result. By putting things off to the last minute, a child is encouraged to delay steps, rush through them, or skip them altogether, which almost invariably produces inferior work.

When your child is faced with a school task or project, guide them by asking the following questions:

- *What would this finished product look like if it were done well?*
- *How long will it take to complete this project in a quality manner?*
- *Would a schedule or timetable help to manage the completion of this project?*
- *How much daily time will be required to complete the project?*

Check your child's progress with him daily and adjust the schedule if necessary.

This may seem cumbersome, but many of us are required to complete projects in this very fashion in our jobs. Helping your child develop the habit of following quality processes will set them up for future success.

Quality Performances

The word *performance* implies a show put on to entertain, educate, or display talent. Yet any form of presentation is also a performance. At some point, most children have to present information to a group of people, maybe even eventually as part of their jobs. The classroom is a good place to practice these performance skills. Interestingly, both products and processes almost always accompany performances. The following questions are for defining and evaluating a quality performance:

- *How well prepared is the student on the subject matter?*
- *Did he stay within the prescribed time limit (if any)?*
- *Did he use a variety of media during the presentation?*
- *Did he engage his audience during the presentation, either by use of a question and answer session or by some other method of participation?*
- *Did he begin with an introduction and end with a conclusion?*
- *Was he enthusiastic about the content of the presentation?*

What Does Quality Look Like?

The most difficult aspect of quality for most of us to understand is what it looks like. We usually know it when we see it. Many students do not produce quality work. Aside from those children who are perfectionists by nature, most children just do the bare minimum to get by. This is not entirely their fault. With the lowering of expectations that infests our schools, sometimes teachers don't require a job that is well done, and many settle for the job's just being done at all! Unfortunately, an *A* doesn't always mean what it used to mean. That's why it's our job as parents to not only encourage our children to do quality work, but to make the idea of a quality job meaningful to them. One way to do this is to change the way you teach them. Instead of just demanding quality, begin to lead them in it by example.

My husband, Chip, loves to help people straighten messy areas in their homes or businesses. In fact, as a space planner and designer he thrives on the jobs you might call "the worst garage you've ever seen." He gets practically giddy if someone calls for fear that they can no longer open a closet door for everything falling out. For him, the messier, the better. Sometimes he takes the boys with him when he organizes a garage. It can be a long, tedious process. On such occasions, the boys get bored easily and often ask, "Isn't this good enough, Dad?" Chip uses the opportunity to teach them about quality. When the job is done, the client is either thrilled, amazed, or impressed—usually all three! Their reaction to Chip's job well done makes a great impression on our sons.

Look first for quality products, processes, and performances in your own life. Let your children see you go through the process of creating or planning something in a quality manner. Then engage their help as often as possible as a way of reinforcing the right way to do something.

Define Quality

Even if your child understands the general idea of quality, you may need to be more specific in your direction. When you say, "Please clean your room," does he know exactly what you mean by that? Or, when he is done, are there still clothes on the floor, the closet door open, and a water glass from the night before still on the nightstand? Take the time to define with your child what your expectation of quality is before you expect it from him. (For more on defining quality, see the family activity at the end of this chapter.)

Is there something you're currently struggling to get your child to do properly? Quality work is something we must watch for and be diligent in teaching and reinforcing. Even though our sons have grown up in a home that has always been quality-minded, they still slip back into bad habits. It's human nature.

For example, the simple task of brushing the dog belongs to our younger child. When I do it, it takes me at least 15 minutes to complete. For some reason, it only takes him two! However, upon inspection of his work, I see that only the surface has been brushed and Leah's fur is still a mess underneath. Speed does not equal quality! Yet in this case, the sloppy work was my fault: Instead of teaching him the right way to do it, I just assumed he knew. Now I know better!

Expect Quality

Teaching quality and expecting it are two different tasks. It's one thing to set the expectation, but following through is another matter. Try to be consistent and pay attention, even though it takes more time to do so. If you teach your child now that you are serious about your expectations, their future employers, spouse, and peers will have you to thank.

It's much easier to do mediocre or poor work. It's hard to do a quality job. But taking the easy way out does nothing to improve our lives. Why should we expect quality from our children? Because it's the quest for improvement that will better their quality of life.

Measure Quality

Now that we know quality when we see it and will expect it from our children and ourselves, how do we maintain it? There are two effective ways to gauge how well we are meeting and exceeding our expectations of quality.

One of the best ways to measure how well your child is doing what he does is by conferencing. My husband and I conference with the boys periodically during what has become known as "just-you-and-me" days. We go out to grab ice cream, breakfast, or some other treat and simply talk about the quality that's being produced in our lives.

We have found that our older son has difficulty finishing the jobs he starts. He begins with good intentions and then either gets distracted or bored and quietly walks away from it. During a "quality conference," we might discuss ways he could do his job without becoming distracted. I usually remind him of the rule in our home that you can't complain about something unless you also have a solution to offer. When our children become involved in this process, they come up with their own ways to improve. That's when you know they're engaged actively in their own quest for quality.

There is one caution I would offer when conferencing about quality: I have found that targeting no more than two quality issues at a time is the best option. We all have a long way to go and listing everything all at once that you want your child to improve upon can be more than a little discouraging. Realize that it took your child a long time to form those bad habits, and it will take a long time to break them.

A second way to measure quality is to keep a record. Teachers use grades, which work in the school environment, but checklists and rubrics are better methods to follow in the home. Monitor your child's quality level by creating a checklist of what things to notice when, for instance, they clean their room. Put this list on a clipboard and either hang it on their bedroom door or hand it to them when it's time for that chore. As they check off each item, both you and your child can have confidence that they've done what was expected. At first, checklists may seem a bit regimented, but they are effective. And if you have a particularly messy or undisciplined child, you'll be glad when you begin to use them!

Essentially, with both of these tactics, we are teaching our children that how well they do things can improve the quality of their life and the lives of those around them. And when they find themselves as teens working at

The Burger Shack with a "quality-control checklist" to fulfill, not only will they be familiar with the concept, but they will know exactly what to expect!

From Competence to Quality

Learning *how* to produce quality work doesn't happen overnight. Yet determining *why* quality is important can be an equally challenging task. Since teachers do not always expect quality, students don't always learn why it's necessary. And even if you expect quality, you may need to give your child time to work up to understanding why quality is important.

Learning why is the first step. Doing competent work follows next. *Competency* means doing what is expected. Once your child can prove that he can do competent work, a commitment to improvement is what will lead to quality.

The formula is:

$$Competence + Improvement = Quality$$

You can encourage this process, but you can't mandate it. Guiding our children to do quality work because it ultimately improves their lives is the reason to do it. Making it more enjoyable should be the goal, and never just "because I say so."

Self-Evaluation

Encourage your child to look at what they've done before claiming that they are finished. They need to be able to say, "This is my best work because…" If they know what's expected and they believe they have done just that, they need to be able to verbalize it. Another way to help children see how well they have done their work is to use a rubric. A rubric is similar to a checklist in that it is a list of skills, but it also includes a rating scale to gauge how well each item was completed.

Here is an example of a rubric for math homework:

S=Student's Assessment   P=Parent's Assessment

Scale: 0 - did not do   1 - did sometimes

            2 - did most of time   3 - did every time

	S	P
Heading	3	3
Complete	3	2
Neat	3	2
Correct	3	3
Showed Work	3	3
Total	15	13

Self-Reflection

After your child grades himself, then it's your turn to rate his work. When you first begin this process, you probably won't agree with your child's self-evaluation. That just goes to show how little children understand what quality work is. Over time you may find that you and your child agree more often than not. Because most children are not used to assessing their own work, helping children take ownership of the kind of work they do ultimately encourages them to be responsible for it. And learning to look objectively at oneself is a skill from which children will benefit down the road.

Self-Improvement

This is the final step in moving your child toward producing quality work. After taking stock of how well he did, he should then take some time to

consider ways he could do better the next time. Household chores are a great opportunity to practice self-improvement. Even your child's homework assignments can usually be improved. When your child reaches a point where he can think of no more ways to improve, quality has been achieved!

Let's say your child has a book report to do. On the continuum from competence to quality, your child may already be at the point of competence. He knows when the report is due and has already started reading the book. He not only understands the requirements, but he also enjoys English class and believes that he can do a great book report if he puts his mind to it. You remind him to make a list of the teacher's expectations to keep at his side as he works so he can know what is expected.

He finishes the report four days before it is due and intends to hand it in early. You ask him to share his report with you and explain why he deserves an *A*, knowing he has come far this year in his abilities, but fearing he may be becoming lazy. You sit down together and your son goes through the report, grading himself on the expectations his teacher put forth. You remind him that in order to improve, he will likely have to fulfill the requirements even better to receive an *A*. You think that a *B* would probably be assigned for this assignment if he only did what was expected so you encourage him to do a little more.

Here is where problems can arise. When teachers accept competent work as *A* work, your child may not agree that his paper is only worth a *B*. After all, the teacher says it's worth an *A*. While his teacher may accept it, you can still help build the missing inspiration and lead him toward *self-improvement*. Remind him that when he enters the world of work and romantic relationships, he will want to be noticed as one who goes above and beyond. Turn the situation into an opportunity by showing the successful results that his high expectations can bring both now and later in life.

Guide your child's understanding of quality by asking the following question: If your child could turn in a little longer report, could he improve on his teacher's expectations? Perhaps the following goals could be set.

Expectations of Teacher

1. Length - two pages
2. Neat writing
3. Main characters named and described in one sentence each
4. Setting described in one sentence
5. Supporting characters listed
6. Plot described in three paragraphs
7. Questions about value and relevancy answered
8. Recommendation to read book given

Improvements

1. Length - 2.5 pages
2. Typed, double-spaced
3. Main characters named and described in two sentences each
4. Setting described in two sentences
5. Supporting characters listed and described
6. Plot described in five paragraphs
7. Questions answered and examples provided
8. Recommendation given and further recommendations made about similar books

When your child works hard to improve the report, he is able to earn an *A* he can be proud of. Competency plus improvement equals quality.

Your Turn to Learn

Before leading your child in the quest for quality, it's important to consider whether you yourself produce quality work. Do you pursue quality in your work, at home, and in your relationships with others? For this assignment, be your own "quality controller." For each statement, determine whether your answer is *true* or *false*.

- I am aware of my strengths and weaknesses.
- I am aware of something in my life that could use improvement and am taking steps to do so.
- I can accept constructive criticism without getting defensive.
- I am confident enough about my job performance to sign my name to anything I do.
- My family and friends can trust me to follow through on my promises.
- I'm aware of when others produce quality and I let them know I've noticed.

Consistently considering the level of quality we are pursuing develops a new self-awareness. Once we have mastered this in ourselves, we can then encourage this awareness in our children and begin laying the foundation for their personal improvement in the future.

Connections

When making the connections between work and quality, we began by looking at the quality of *products, processes,* and *performances.* Take action now by introducing your child to these requirements for quality—at home and beyond.

✔ Home

(Performance) Chores are one of the best training grounds for the early development of quality. You should always expect a job well done! Make sure that you express the things you require for doing a quality job, and that the chores you assign are appropriate for both the child's age and ability.

> *Show & Tell:* Let your children see how you do your own chores. Tell them you sometimes do chores you dislike, yet explain that you still try to do them well.

✔ School

(Process) Homework and special projects are intended to lead a student from following a quality process that will lead to a quality product. Make sure your child has the time she needs to do a quality job. If she's too rushed to do a good job, she's too busy and needs to eliminate other responsibilities or activities.

> *Show & Tell*: Do you do some of your own work at home? Do you have lessons or a study group for which you prepare at home? Are you taking a class or are you involved in some other kind of "homework"? Let your children see what you do to improve.

✔ Work

(Performance) Is your child ready for a part-time job? If it's mowing the neighbor's lawn, talk about the expectation of quality. If it's stocking shelves or working with customers at the local grocery store, he'll need to find out what the manager considers quality work, and then go beyond those expectations.

> *Show & Tell*: What are your expectations of quality in your job? What do you do when you notice someone else hasn't done quality work? If a repairman leaves a mess at your house, or a waitress has

an attitude and brings cold food, use these to show your children examples of poor quality. But be sure to provide positive examples as well, pointing out that some workers do remember details and perform their jobs with pride.

Family Activity

This activity will help you teach the concept of *quality* to your children in a fun and memorable way. And it tastes great too! Use the application points to help connect the idea of quality to other areas of your child's life.

Cookie Quality Test

Materials Needed: Five different brands of chocolate chip cookies, placed in plastic bags and numbered so only you know which is which.

1. First, tell your child something like this: "Many different brands on the market claim to be the best, but today we're going to find out for ourselves." Explain that these same tests are how cookie makers measure the quality of their products. Good tests always include both subjective and objective measurements. If necessary, explain the terms *objective* and *subjective*. For a test to be objective, it must be *blind*—but not all blind tests are objective. For instance, taste is nearly always subjective. Then tell your child that he is now going to determine which cookie is of the highest quality.

2. Ask the children to simply look at the different cookies and have them create a list of criteria for the cookie quality test (these might include taste, ingredients, number of chips, aroma, size, shape, color, etc.)

3. Create a rubric [see sample given in chapter] to rank each criteria on the list. Taste may be included, but should be in the subjective category. Taste will probably carry a lot of weight in the decision of quality, yet you should explain that it is one of the most subjective criteria. Explain that

this makes judging quality difficult because everyone has different taste preferences.

4. Have your child rate each criteria from 1 to 5 in quality points (5 representing the highest quality and 1 the lowest) as you examine and taste each cookie.

5. Go down the list, rating each cookie, and calculate its points. From the total, rank each cookie from lowest to highest number of quality points.

6. Discuss the testing process and whether some criteria are more sub-jective or less, and whether it was worthwhile to consider the criteria you did. Finally, discuss why successful cookie makers feel it is worthwhile to be concerned about quality.

For further application: You may have found that each of you had different ideas of what made quality cookies. Begin by discussing why it is important to be as objective as possible when deciding on quality, then discuss what attributes contribute to the quality of the following things:

- A book
- A report or project
- A home
- A car

An Independent Learner

"Wisdom is supreme; therefore get wisdom.
Though it cost all you have, get understanding."
—PROVERBS 4:7

When you homeschool your children, you try to get household chores done at the same time, which leaves more time for children to work independently on their studies. We homeschooled our children for four years, and I worked hard to help my children become independent workers. When they were doing an assignment, I would throw in a load of laundry, dust, or even vacuum. I got to the point where I knew it took 31 seconds for me to walk from the table to the laundry room to switch the clothes from the washer to the dryer!

Our firstborn could work independently from the start. By the fourth grade he had started his schoolwork even before I woke up in the morning and stayed focused as long as it took for him to complete his assignments. However, our youngest, Charles, took a little longer to learn to work independently.

There was a time when I couldn't make the short trip to the laundry room fast enough for Charles. Every time I'd try, he would disappear! One minute he'd be working quietly on his spelling, the next he'd be off somewhere else. What was he doing? He'd either be in the living room petting the dog, in the family room staring out the skylight, in his room playing superheroes, or something else equally exasperating. Worse, it was a daily occurrence.

It took some time—and a leveled threat of punishment—to get Charles to stay on task. It was a matter of training and required a great deal of structure and consistency. We encouraged him to develop self-control, determination, and perseverance, all personal qualities necessary before any progression in his schoolwork would take place.

By the time a child reaches the seventh or eighth grade, he is expected to be able to work independently on schoolwork. However, learning to work independently doesn't happen at school. Teachers have no time to teach these skills—yet with a little time and effort, we can foster these habits at home.

Independent Learners Are Self-Directed

At the end of the first quarter of the school year, my son's first middle-school report card arrived home. He did quite well except for a *B* in math. It wasn't that I expected him to get straight *A*s, but according to the papers he'd brought home, he should have.

"What happened?" I asked. "I thought you had an *A*."

"I missed a quiz that day we had the pizza party," he told me.

"You mean you didn't know about it in time to make it up?" I asked, reaching for the phone to call his teacher.

"No," he hesitated. "I knew. I just never figured out how to make it up."

I hung up the phone in disappointment. My son hadn't taken the time to ask his teacher what to do when he missed an assignment. And whether or not his teacher had sufficiently explained the policy, he hadn't sought out the answer he needed.

School isn't the only place this happens.

For Christopher, it happened soon after in another setting. It was Sunday and because he and his father were both suffering from food poisoning, we stayed home from church. Little did I know that it was Christopher's week to volunteer in the three-year-old Sunday-school classroom. Later that day, when the child-care supervisor called to ask why Christopher hadn't shown up, I saw the look of horror cross my son's face when he realized that other people had been counting on his presence.

Knowing what to do when you're absent is part of being responsible, and a big part of becoming independent. Parents need to help their children consider whether or not they are ready for a particular responsibility. Have they had enough exposure and practice to know what the right thing to do is and how to do it? That day I learned that my son wasn't prepared for the responsibility of working in the child-care department, but I also realized that I had never addressed it with him. By using that disappointment as a teachable moment, we both learned a bit more of what it takes to develop as responsibly minded, independent learners.

There will be many chances to learn new skills and then apply them to everyday life. If children don't grasp the idea that they themselves are the ones responsible for their actions, they may wonder why opportunities always seem to pass them by. We need to make sure they aren't sitting on the sidelines waiting for life to happen to them. They must learn to make choices and be responsible about the choices they make.

Independent Learners Know What They Need

Along with your child's teacher, cultivate your child's self-awareness of his own needs in every area of life. Is he aware that his learning at school connects with his present and future life? Children don't often see these connections and teachers don't usually have time to help them. We've all complained about learning particular skills until we realize their usefulness in our everyday lives. I know I felt that way about algebra! Parents need to help their children see how everything they are learning at home and at school will connect to life beyond the classroom.

Recently, my husband helped Christopher make a relevant connection during one of his weekly chores.

"The vacuum isn't picking much up," Christopher complained.

"Why do you think that is?" Chip asked.

"I don't know. Can you fix it?" Christopher asked.

"Yes," Chip said. "But I won't. Get a new bag and I'll show you how."

Christopher retrieved a new vacuum bag from the closet and held it out to his father.

"The instructions are right there. Go ahead."

"But I've never done it before. Can't you do it for me?" Christopher whined.

"Nope. Learn now so that when you get married your wife won't think you're totally useless," Chip said, smiling at him, and throwing me a sly glance from across the kitchen.

"What's the big deal?" Christopher said. "It's just a vacuum."

"Today it's a vacuum, tomorrow it's a lawn mower, and later, it will be your kid's bicycle that needs fixing. Learn now and do yourself a favor," Chip said.

After several failed attempts, Christopher fitted the new bag correctly and the vacuum whirred to life to finish the job.

As Christopher was putting the vacuum back in the closet, Chip gave him a final quiz. "So how will you know the next time you need a new bag?"

"When it's not sucking anything up anymore," Christopher said. "And don't worry. It won't take me three tries to put the bag in next time."

My husband is quite capable. He says it's because his father wasn't handy around the house and it was up to him and his brothers to learn those things on their own. Thankfully, he did have help from his grandfather in learning how to build, repair, and maintain things, and his mother taught him how to help around the house. I am personally quite grateful to his mother and grandfather because I was able to marry a man who does whatever is necessary to take care of his home and his children.

Sometimes it can be tempting to do everything yourself. It's faster, and you can usually do a better job. But you do your child a disservice when you do it all yourself. Take the time now to teach him how to care for his needs and the needs of others—the few extra minutes are worth it.

Another simple way to encourage independence is to teach your child how to use a dictionary. It's one of the first tools they can use to find information on their own. It's also a skill that's largely lost in today's typical elementary education. As a kid, it didn't take me long to discover that if I wanted to know something, I had to look it up for myself. My mother, who loved language and books, always said, "Look it up!" It used to frustrate me to stop what I was doing to find the dictionary, but I began to learn that when I wanted an answer, I could find it myself.

Of course, birth-order studies tell us that firstborns are usually more responsible, self-directed learners. Does that mean that a middle child, or the youngest, cannot learn? Of course not! It does, however, mean that you may have to work a little harder to get your child to see the relevance in a particular activity. You may have to give him a little more guidance when it comes to finding out how to do something for himself, but don't give up. If he makes you work a little harder, show him he's worth every minute!

Later, when it comes time to apply to colleges or find a job, your teenager will be able to find out what steps are necessary to achieve his goal. Your goal as a parent is to work yourself right out of a job! Any flight instructor knows he must eventually hand over the controls if he wants his student to learn to fly on his own. We're here to give our children their own wings, not carry them around on ours.

Independent Learners Set Specific and Realistic Personal Goals

Goal-setting isn't just for corporate boardrooms. Start teaching your child this important skill with goals that relate directly to home or school, such as, "I will be able to do my chores without being reminded," or "I will remember to write down what my homework is every day." Guide your children as they set goals, and then help them reach them. There are three kinds of goals you can focus on for both yourself and your children: academic goals, process goals, and character goals.

Academic goals are just what the name entails—goals involving formal education. In what subjects can your children improve? Are they starting a new class such as a foreign language or calculus or drama? One academic goal might be, "I will master my times tables," or "I will memorize my geometry theorems." Setting academic goals now can translate into job-related goals later: "I will master the office procedures quickly," or "I will memorize the dinner menu and the specials for the day."

Process goals are goals that focus on *how* you do something. Such goals might include, "I will finish my homework *in a timely manner*," or "I will do my math homework *neatly*." Think of adverbs (or words ending in *-ly*) to describe *how* you do something.

Character goals describe the attitude with which we do our work. For example, "I will *persevere* through my math homework even when it's difficult," or "I will *stop complaining* about my English teacher," are both character goals. You may have heard it said that attitude is everything, and it's true. Without a good attitude, even if you do your job perfectly, employers still may not be pleased with your performance.

Begin by setting goals for yourself in these three areas. Currently my own personal goals are to complete a one-on-one Bible study with a close friend, file things from my "in basket" in a timely manner (which would still not be fast enough for my husband!), and tell my boys more often how much I enjoy them (it gets harder to do that when they are preteens). Let your children know the goals you are setting for yourself. It will be easier to encourage them to reach their goals if they've seen you do it yourself.

Independent Learners Self-Monitor Progress to Stay Motivated

My goal for this weekend was to finish one chapter in this book. I planned to write five pages per day. Every five pages I wrote gave me more and more satisfaction. It encouraged me to continue—even when I didn't feel like it. Help your child do the same with their homework, a long project, or another activity. *Determination* is the key quality!

Linda Kavelin Popov describes determination this way: "Determination is focusing your energy and efforts on a particular task and then sticking with it until it is done. Determination is using your will-power to do something even when it isn't easy."[1] Many children have somehow learned that they only need to put effort into the things they *like* to do. But how often does that really happen? In your own job, whether you work in or out of the home, there are plenty of tasks that you don't like to do. But children need to see our determination to do these tasks and do them well, even when we don't want to.

Things just don't get done unless we're determined to do them. For some gifted children, things come almost too easily. They don't learn how to persevere because they didn't have to in order to get the grade they desired. These children need more challenging goals in order for them to gain determination. For others, they have tried and failed so often that they've actually given up. They see no value in perseverance because their tasks or goals are too overwhelming for them. When I taught learning-disabled students, I had a classroom full of children with broken spirits. It's hard to remain determined when you're stuck in a cycle of failure. These children need a supportive environment both at home and at school. They also need goals that are set within their reach, especially until they gain confidence and determination. But both gifted and slower children require our help to stay focused, to keep going when the task gets difficult, and to believe what they're doing is important for their own futures.

Independent Learners Respond Positively to Feedback

My husband and I try to have non-threatening "conferences" with our boys periodically to see how they're doing with the goals they have set for themselves. Once a child has learned how to set goals and monitor his progress toward those goals, he is more open to hearing ways he can improve his performance. Go out for ice cream or to another favorite place to talk about it. The key is to teach them how to accept constructive criticism without getting defensive.

Most importantly, you must teach your child to have *self-control* in her response so that she can receive help from others. When a parent, teacher, or employer gives your child feedback, she needs to be able to respond in an unemotional manner and be as objective as possible. When she is able to separate her feelings from the facts, she will be able to see the validity in what others have noticed and learn from it.

I face this every time I receive a rejection letter from a publisher. Most do not offer feedback when they turn down a manuscript, but sometimes they give feedback in the form of criticism—constructive and otherwise! Feedback is always valuable if I can control my desire to become defensive or emotional. When I can sift through criticism and see the helpful insights, I am always better for having done so.

Independent Learners Are Steadfast and Diligent

Another quality of an independent learner is *steadfastness*. This is more than just making a commitment to something. Steadfastness could be called "determination with heart." It is a constant attitude of being dependable, faithful, and committed, no matter what the obstacle. Steadfastness is a rare quality to find, especially in children. All people waver. All people wander. But willfully committing your heart and mind to the things and people that truly matter in life is a quality every independent learner must have to succeed. There will always be obstacles, and we will all experience doubt. But when we are steadfast, we don't have to be derailed from the track.

Diligence is another defining characteristic of an independent learner. The opposite of diligence is laziness. It can be a struggle to get our children to take responsibility, but diligence is the thing most needed because it shows your child it's worth the effort. If we begin to notice an attitude of laziness, we must investigate its true cause. It might be that your child's learning environment is either too easy or too difficult. The goal is to set our children up to succeed. Success leads to success, so if we can lead them by our own example one step at a time, they will succeed—with their spirits intact.

Independent Learners Address Problems as They Arise

How does your child respond to the problems or challenges he encounters in his life? Can your child come up with a step-by-step plan to solve a problem? Or does he whine and complain, or sit silently, hoping it will just go away? If the problem is that he has done something wrong, he may be having trouble accepting the repercussions, and he might make excuses instead of admitting his mistake. You can tell that a child has not learned to deal with problems when his chronic answer to the question, "What are you going to do about it?" is "I don't know." I have an "I-don't-know" kid. Do you?

Sometimes we need to provide the actual words for our children to use for a given situation. For example, what does your child say to his sibling if he's hurt his feelings (or his body!)? The most common response is "I'm sorry." But in order for a child to learn to take responsibility for his actions, the words, "Please forgive me for hurting you," are more appropriate. The words, "I'm sorry," can mean "I'm sorry you're hurt," not, "I'm sorry I did something wrong." There should be some sort of admission of guilt and validation of the other person's feelings. Consider what you say to your spouse or child if you've wronged them. Do you yourself take personal responsibility for that hurt, or do you place the blame somewhere else?

Sometimes the "problem" our children face is being confronted about their beliefs and opinions. For them to be able to stand up and declare what they believe, they must be able to offer evidence for those beliefs. Parents must teach that it takes more than just saying no to something they know to be wrong. Are they able and willing to tell the person the reason behind their decision? They should be prepared because they will be confronted at some point in their lives.

Independent Learners Hold an Independent Point of View

We all want our children to be able to stand up for what they believe, even when we are not around. Did your mother ever ask you, "Would you go jump off a bridge if So-and-So told you to"? We hope that our children

will do what is right regardless of what everyone else is doing. We want them to be able to speak their minds even if it means a loss of popularity.

Leadership often entails having an independent point of view. We have two boys: Christopher is more of a leader, and Charles is more of a follower. They are the first- and lastborn respectively. Does this mean Charles is doomed to always be a follower, never able to stand up for what is right? Does this mean that Christopher will always do what is right regardless of what others do? Not at all. These are only tendencies, and both require a continuous dialogue. Chip and I need to encourage Charles to do the right thing in all circumstances and make sure Christopher knows what it means to be a competent leader. There are children who are leaders, and there are children who are followers. Do you know which your children are?

What things does your family practice or believe that contradict the world around you? Is it difficult for you to stand firmly on what you believe in front of your colleagues, your friends, or even your extended family? Are you easily swayed? Are you double-minded? These are all issues you may have to deal with in yourself before you can successfully address them with your children.

In the end, being an independent learner really comes down to being responsible. In her book *Family Virtues*, Linda Kavelin Popov defines responsibility this way: "Being responsible means that others can depend on you...[it] means to do something well and to the best of your ability...[it] is being willing to be accountable for what you do or don't do. When you are responsible, you keep your agreements. When you make a mistake, you take responsibility for it. Being responsible is a sign of growing up."[2]

And that should be what we all desire for our children.

✎ Your Turn to Learn

How do you rate as an independent learner? Check off all the qualities that apply to you from the list below. In which areas do you need to improve to provide a good model for your child?

- I do every job to the best of my ability until it is completed.
- I keep my agreements with others and work to clear up any misunderstandings.
- I focus on my own responsibilities, not someone else's.
- I am willing to accept praise or correction when appropriate.
- I admit my mistakes without giving excuses.
- I take on new responsibilities at a level I can handle.
- When I am not prepared or able to take something on, I say so.
- I look for opportunities to use my abilities.
- I do what is expected when no one is checking up on me.
- I take initiative to get my work done in an orderly manner.
- I don't let doubts or trials blow me off course in accomplishing my goals.
- I pace myself at a rate I can maintain.

It's easy to see only what we want to see about ourselves. If you're brave, you may want to ask someone else—an objective observer—to consider this inventory with you.

Connections

No matter what their future career choice may be, your child's success depends on their becoming an independent learner. Support this trait by modeling independence and look for age-appropriate ways to "let go" and allow your child to fly unassisted.

✔ Home

Home is the safest place to try out new wings. As you assign chores, make sure your child is (1) capable of completing the task, (2) given a specific time frame in which to complete it, and (3) clear about his responsibility. Start small, but begin to give your child more and more responsibility as he gets older. By the time he's ready to leave for college, he'll know how to take care of himself.

Show & Tell: Do you finish the jobs you start around the house? Do you take your responsibility seriously? When you need help do you ask for it? Let your child see how you do things and show them what responsible forward-thinking requires.

✔ School

Since your child's teacher probably doesn't have time to ensure that every child is staying on task and completing all assigned work, you should work with your child and his teacher to make sure this takes place.

Show & Tell: When communicating with your child's teacher, nurture that relationship so that the teacher can in turn nurture her relationship with your child. Make sure your children know that you support their teachers' decisions. Encourage them to persevere, even when it's tough.

✔ Work

Employers seek employees who are self-starters—people who don't wait around to be told what to do or how to do it. This is a highly valued trait that directly leads to success in business. Even when your child takes that seasonal job at the local Renaissance Festival, encourage him to be a "dream employee."

Show & Tell: Do you have goals for your own job and future? Are you "pressing toward the mark?" Share those dreams with your children. Let them get caught up in your excitement!

Family Activity

Independence requires initiative. Employers value initiative-takers because they are both good for business and for relationships. Below are five scenarios that can be used to encourage initiative. Write each on a slip of paper and then have each family member pick one. Let each person read his scenario aloud, describing what he or she thinks should be done. Discuss whether or not their answer shows initiative. Then allow other family members to add their own ideas as well.

- Your room is a mess, and company is coming very soon.
- You have been sick for three days and have missed a lot of homework assignments.
- Mom has had surgery and has been in the hospital for a week. She is coming home today.
- Your partner for your group project is not helping, and your project is due in one week.
- You discover you are out of shampoo in your bathroom.

Chapter Four

A Creative Thinker

"The man who thinks he knows something
does not yet know as he ought to know."
—1 CORINTHIANS 8:2

It was my first drawing class, and I was already threatened by the assignment of drawing circles. My dad is an artist. My younger brother is an artist. But the blank page intimidated me, just staring back, egging me on to fail. My newly sharpened pencil hung in the air, full of intention, frozen in fear. It seemed that no matter how hard I tried, I could never seem to draw with any precision or ease. I believed I just wasn't creative. It wouldn't have been so hard otherwise, would it have?

My attempts at drawing circles were laughable. I couldn't bear for anyone else in the class to see them. I thought I could even hear the page itself laughing at me. *What's the point?* I remember thinking. *There's no way I can ever be like my brother or my dad. Why should I even try?*

Do you believe you are creative? I've since found out that many people feel inadequate in this area, but it's usually simply because we don't understand what creativity really is. Without creativity there would be no advancements, no new innovations or inventions. According to Dorothy

Sisk, an educational psychology professor at Lamar University, "Creativity is a precious commodity, and creative people are the ones who will make the great advances in medicine and science, literature and art and move our civilization forward."[1]

Creative thinkers possess special tools for defining and solving problems. When evaluating the choices before them, they know how to consider all possible effects and outcomes. And they have the ability to evaluate multiple alternatives and develop plans for adjusting their response to those evaluations.

What Is Creativity?

My friend Diane has children the same age as mine. One day when our children were very young, she came to me, distraught: "I need help! Do you have any books on arts and crafts?"

Diane is a very capable person and a great mother, but she was in a panic that particular day because it had suddenly struck her that her children weren't going to be creative—because she herself wasn't creative.

"How can my children learn to be creative?" she exclaimed. "I'm not creative at all! I'm good at following instructions, though. Do you have something with instructions?"

I told her that I did, but I also told her she was mistaken. She *was* creative; she just wasn't *artistic*. The difference between the two is huge.

Creativity is the power of imagination. Everyone has the ability to see old things in new ways, to do things in ways that have never been tried before. In her book *The Family Virtues Guide*, Linda Kavelin Popov puts it this way: "When we share our ideas . . . things can be improved. When scientists are creative, they come up with new cures for diseases. Every person can serve the world by learning about arts and sciences."[2] Creativity is a natural ability we all possess. Each of us has been given different gifts and talents that we need to discover, but creativity is an inborn reflection of the universal creativity all around us.

One component of creativity is the ability to think of unique ways to make things work better. Most improvement—of anything—requires creative thinking. We can think creatively by employing four basic qualities: fluency, flexibility, originality, and sensitivity.

Fluency

Fluency refers to a deep understanding of and capability to use a certain language or system. If someone is fluent in creativity, it means he can generate a large number of ideas when confronting a problem or seeking improvements. This ability could also be seen as *creative agility*. Much creative thought requires remaining detached enough from any one idea to allow others to be considered. This may not come naturally to us, especially if we are used to censoring our ideas, as most of us are. Some of us have so brutally censored our ideas, we agonize over coming up with just one original thought. But from us our children also learn that there is only one right answer—and they will search for that one, and when they find it, they quit. A child who has learned to think this way is likely to feel unsafe and panic when offered the freedom to come up with numerous ideas.

In his book *How Creative Are You?* Eugene Raudsepp offers various exercises to demonstrate creative strategies.[3] Try this one:

Test your fluency by naming at least 12 possible uses for sunglasses.

Examples: To protect eyes from sunlight glare. To hide a black eye. To hide the fact that you're not wearing makeup. To change your appearance. To cut something. To hide your hearing aid. To look like a movie star. To look like you're blind. To use as a mirror. To hold your hair back. To protect your eyes from dust or smog. To relieve a headache caused by a glare. To use as a paperweight. To chew on during long meetings.

Admittedly, some of your ideas might seem silly at first, but remember, the object is to allow yourself to generate as many ideas as possible—both the silly and the solid. Sometimes the perfect solution to your problem is hiding among the silly answers!

Flexibility

The creative thinker is able to choose and explore a *variety* of approaches and options to his problem, without losing sight of his overall goal. When one line of thought comes to a dead end, creative thinkers can easily take up another. My husband calls this "rolling with the punches." When I was growing up, if my family's plan about where to go to dinner or how to accomplish a task didn't work, it was over! It wasn't until I married a flexible husband that I found out you can have a plan B, or even plans C, D, or E for that matter. Flexibility is evident when you can perceive a problem from *multiple* viewpoints to increase your options.

Let's go back to the exercise we just did and consider how many *different* answers there are. Each verb will indicate the approach.

Test your flexibility by naming at least 12 different uses for sunglasses.

Examples: *Protect* eyes from sunlight, glare, dust, and smog. *Hide* a black eye, lack of makeup, or a hearing aid. *Change* appearance. *Use* to cut something, as a mirror, or as a paperweight. *Look* like a movie star or a blind person. *Hold* hair back. *Relieve* a headache. *Chew* on during meetings.

Did you count eight?

Originality

Creative thinking requires originality, commonly referred to as "thinking outside the box." Original thinkers create new combinations and new relationships. They reach beyond established systems and ignore accepted boundaries.

Of course, we know there are no truly original ideas. But there are degrees of originality with which ideas can be compared to others. Original thinking can be an exhausting exercise of the mind. It's not easy to be atypical.

A fun way to practice your original thinking skills is to play the game *Scattergories*. The goal is to come up with as many original ideas within a given category as possible. The activity at the end of this chapter gives a fun way to encourage creative thinking such as this.

To be an original thinker, all you need to do is oppose, change, or complement what people normally expect. But don't expect original ideas to go unchallenged. Often they are pronounced impractical, infeasible, or unacceptable.

Sensitivity

Remaining sensitive helps direct creative thinkers. We all operate on different levels of sensitivity. Some of us are *overly sensitive* and our constant awareness of impending problems can overwhelm and even paralyze us. Some of us are *insensitive* and even the most obvious clues to potential crises don't register. Learning a balance between these two extremes is invaluable to the creative thought process.

In order to set realistic goals, we must be sensitive to and realistic about the problems that surround us. We have worldwide problems, family problems, problems with friends, and individual problems. Creative thinkers find solutions by first becoming aware of the true magnitude of the problem. For children, a good place to start learning this skill is by practicing putting themselves in another's place.

Doris Shallcross, author of *Teaching Creative Behavior*, says that developing sensitivity to problems is largely *predicting* them by reading the clues as to what might happen. This ensures that the child is not merely passively *reacting* to a given problem. Remaining sensitive to potential problems is a central component to a child's ability to put herself in another's place. Do

the following exercise first with yourself and then with your children to develop better problem sensitivity.

Mentally picture a peaceful country scene or a quiet city street early in the morning.

Then predict what problems might erupt within a few hours or what problems might already exist, but of which you may be currently unaware.

When you use this exercise with young children, choose a scene that is familiar to them, such as their schoolyard, their backyard, or their Sunday-school classroom.

Fear: Barrier to Creative Thought

Unfortunately, most of us face a formidable barrier to our creative thought: the barrier of *fear*. In his book *How Creative Are You?* Eugene Raudsepp describes creativity that is squelched by fear as "a gutter under the eaves of a roof, clogged with dead leaves, twigs, bugs and sediment. In order for the rainwater to flow through, the gutter must first be cleared. In a similar way, free-flowing creativity and receptivity to new ideas also require the elimination of personal and environmental sediments."[4]

We are afraid of appearing different from those around us, so we are cautious with our ideas. We're afraid of humiliation, rejection, isolation, and dishonor. If someone were to say our idea was silly, we would risk losing the respect of those around us. If someone were to say our idea was too odd or unusual, we might find ourselves isolated or shut out. If someone were to think our idea was too controversial, we could lose the respect of a loved one or a friend. Not all of these fears are unfounded. There is risk involved in thinking creatively. We should always count the cost, but when healthy caution turns into abject fear, it can become a formidable obstacle to creative thinking. Our fears are bad habits that need to be broken in order to allow creative thought to flow freely.

Creative Problem Solving

Once we learn that we all have the ability to be creative and we have removed the barrier of fear, we can begin to harness the power of our creativity to solve problems—from the everyday to the worldwide.

The Center for Creative Learning offers workshops and materials about Creative Problem Solving (CPS). According to their Web site "CPS links your natural creativity and problem-solving approaches. It is an easy-to-learn process that can be readily applied by individuals and groups of many ages, in many organizations, settings, and cultures."[5] Creativity sometimes appears to be a random and chaotic activity, but CPS offers structure. It is a process in which we can take the emotion out of the problem at hand and solve it in a step-by-step manner.

Because I have made CPS an ingrained habit through conscious practice, by now I use CPS almost unconsciously. It was a skill I learned in graduate school, then used with my students, and now use with my own children. When faced with a difficult problem, I have learned to automatically follow the steps. Usually I will follow the process in my head, but sometimes, if it's a particularly big or complicated problem, I still write the steps out on paper. If we can teach our children to systematically follow these steps to solve problems now, it will help them form new habits of thinking and be more effective problem-solvers in the future.

Here are the four basic steps to follow when encouraging creative problem solving in your child:

1. Define the problem.

Sometimes defining the actual problem can be the hardest part. It is often difficult to put our finger on exactly what is wrong, especially when we're upset and our emotions are clouding the issue. When that happens, learn to write the whole mess down, calm down, and then try to see the real problem within the mess.

2. Evaluate all possible solutions.

Brainstorm possible solutions or alternatives. List everything that comes to mind, and later judge them according to whether or not they are capable of solving your problem. This is where your creative juices have a chance to flow. Remember, don't censor your ideas—just let them come. The most improbable solution sometimes ends up being the best.

3. Develop a plan of action.

Choose the *most logical* solution—not necessarily the one you like best! Then make a plan of action based on that choice. Form a step-by-step method of implementing your solution. Do you need more facts about the situation before proceeding? Do you need to talk to someone else for advice? What materials do you need? Once you're ready, put your solution into action and see if it works the way you expected.

4. Adjust plans when necessary.

Did the solution that you chose work out the way you had hoped? If not, go back to your list of solutions, choose another, and try again. Sometimes our ideal solution doesn't work. Be willing to make a plan B and try again.

This approach works with almost any problem. When you're learning the process, it's best to start with a smaller personal problem, and then move on to bigger and more far-reaching problems when you've got the knack. Try to define the problem by beginning with the phrase: "In what way(s) might I . . . "

" . . . get my son to school on time?"

" . . . find a reliable babysitter?"

" . . . get my children to do their chores?"

Children's problems can be handled the same way: "In what ways might I . . . be able to pay more attention and not miss the teacher's instructions?" This method helps children face their problems, both big and small, without panicking. When they're young, the stakes may not be as high and the consequences may not be severe. Now is the time to help them learn to think for themselves and embrace the problems of life as opportunities to learn.

✎ Your Turn to Learn

By now you should understand that there is a difference between being *artistic* and being *creative*. Creativity begins in the mind before it is manifested as something you produce. We *can* solve problems with creativity. We *can* come up with new ideas and innovations with creative thought. The only thing that really stops us is fear.

Consider some of the ways we criticize creative thinking in others and ourselves. Then consider some ways you can encourage creative thought.

Criticism of Creative Thought	**Encouragement of Creative Thought**
"It won't work."	"Good going!"
"We don't have the time."	"I like that."
"What will others think?"	"Your brain is in gear today."
"I just know it won't work."	"That's very resourceful."
"That's not our problem."	"That's coming along nicely."
"Let's discuss it some other time."	"You're really talented."
"That's too modern."	"Good thinking!"
"That's too old-fashioned."	"You're learning fast."

Connections

We all face problems—most of us on a daily basis. Whether our children are at home, in school, or at work, they will be challenged to solve problems. Why not help them start applying some creativity to their ability to solve them?

✔ Home

"How can we take care of a stray kitten without bringing him inside?" "In what ways might we raise money for a junior-high mission trip?" "In what

ways might I get along with my younger sister better?" These are all real-life problems kids face at home. They are also all worthy of being managed through Creative Problem Solving.

Show & Tell: "How should I find a reliable babysitter?" "In what ways might I get my children to do their chores?" "How could I lower my grocery bill next month?" Take the time to work through these problems, making sure to include your children in the process.

✔ School

Unfortunately, school can be a breeding ground for problems. Here are just a few to consider solving in a systematic manner: "How can I make new friends at my new school?" "How can I improve my science grade?" Or, "How can I find time to be on the soccer team and still maintain my grades?"

Show & Tell: Parents can be just as involved with the problems that school generates as teachers are. How do you handle a difficult teacher? How do you deal with a disappointing report card from your child? Deal with these issues in a way that separates the emotion from the problem.

✔ Work

Your child will eventually want to earn his own money. Finding a job that allows him to make money but doesn't adversely affect his schoolwork or the family dynamics is a challenge. He'll face this again when he's in college. He'll face it yet again when he maintains a career while raising a family.

Show & Tell: Has your own job ever had a negative impact on your family life? Have you been able to address that issue or have you avoided it? If you have addressed it, explain to your child how you solved the problem. But if not, take responsibility and solve this mushrooming problem now, before the damage is too extensive to reverse.

Family Activity

Creative problem solving is one of the most valuable life skills we can teach our children. As a family, consider the problem below[6] and go through the steps to solve it. Then identify a problem in your own life that as a family you can solve together.

Homesickness

You are at summer camp for the first time. Although you have never been to this camp before, you were excited about the opportunity. For months, you looked forward to your two weeks here, and you are not disappointed when you arrive. The camp is everything it was advertised to be. It's large, very beautiful, and has every sport and recreation facility you could ask for, but . . .

The trouble starts after the third day. Even though you have made several new friends, you are starting to miss your old friends from home. You like the other people assigned to your cabin, but the bunk bed just isn't like your bed at home. You miss your parents and surprisingly, even your brother or sister! Since you have never been away from home for any long period of time before, these feelings are new for you. None of your camp friends seem to be homesick—they're actually *happy* to be away from home. You don't want them to know that you're homesick; they might make things worse.

What will you do? There is still a week and a half left at camp, and even though you are already so homesick you want to leave, you can't admit it to anyone. What will be your plan for the rest of the camp session?

Chapter Five

A Critical Thinker

"Brothers, stop thinking like children.
In regard to evil be infants, but in your thinking be adults."
—1 CORINTHIANS 14:20

U se your brain," I heard my husband say to our oldest son. He wasn't being mean, he was just trying to get Christopher to evaluate the situation. At our house, the boys have their own shower—which includes their own soap, towels, shampoo, and toothpaste. Upon inspection after Christopher's shower, my husband, Chip, noticed that his son's hair was still full of shampoo. Upon closer inspection, he realized it wasn't shampoo—it was actually *soap*!

"Why did you use soap to wash your hair?" Chip asked.

"We're out of shampoo," Christopher said, still dripping.

"How long have you been out of shampoo?" Chip's face showed how baffled he was by this apparent lack of common sense.

"I don't know, maybe a couple of weeks." Christopher stared at his father.

Chip's head raised and he closed his eyes. If he was counting to 10,

I wouldn't have doubted it. This wasn't the first time this had happened.

"Well, next time," Chip spoke slowly, "what do you think you should do when you run out of shampoo?"

Christopher ventured a guess. "Tell you?"

"That's a start. Any other ideas?"

"Umm, put it on the shopping list?" Now the wheels were turning!

"Anything else?" Chip asked.

"Check before I get in the shower?" Christopher's face lit up. "Get some from your bathroom?"

"That's right! Do you think you can remember that?" Chip asked.

"I might need some help," Christopher admitted.

"Don't worry. You'll get it." Chip handed Christopher a new bottle of shampoo and playfully swatted his backside back to the showers.

He was a man of deductive reasoning. What does this phrase mean? The ability to reason is one of the fundamental aspects of being human—we don't operate strictly on unconscious instinct. Reason is the foundation of critical thinking skills.

According to *Webster's Dictionary, reasoning* means to "argue or discuss; to think out logically; to conclude or infer."[1] Logic is the key component to this process. Reasoning entails analysis, deliberation, discernment, evidence gathering, judging, and rationalizing. These could also be synonyms for critical thinking.

Discernment is an important ability in this process. However, it can be easy to forget, especially in today's world. Truth can sometimes seem elusive and relative. It can be dangerous to stand firm on what we know to be true, but it is ultimately more dangerous to ignore it.

Critical Thinkers Analyze Problems and Generate Supporting Arguments

Playing the devil's advocate is one way to develop critical thought processes. Looking at each side of the issue objectively and providing an argument is an ability that requires patience, maturity, and above all, practice. Obstacles to making effective arguments result from errors in reason. Learning how to recognize and remove obstacles to arguments is necessary before learning how to evaluate the arguments themselves.

Children may have trouble recognizing the truth. It's not that they are dishonest (although certainly some may have picked this trait up from adults), it's that they don't always know what the truth is in a given situation. The following "flaws" have been adapted from Vincent Ruggiero's book *The Art of Thinking*.[2] Use them to help teach your children about critical thinking. You may even recognize some of them in yourself.

Either/Or Thinking

"I have to play my video game now because I won't have time later." Children often see things in only black or white. It's all-or-nothing. There is no compromise. Talking them through this thinking can be helpful. Help them see the reality of compromise. Their future spouse will thank you.

Avoiding the Issue

"Why is your brother crying?"

"He was going to knock down my castle."

"I'm not asking you what he did. What did you do to him?"

"He—"

"No. Start with *I*."

"I pushed him."

"Why did you push him?"

"He—"

"Start with *I*."

"I saw that he was about to knock down my castle."

This situation is much easier to resolve when all those concerned face *their own* issues head on and take responsibility. Training children to begin their sentences with *I*, not *he* or *she,* shifts the blame onto what's really happening: *you* are having an argument, so *you* must find a way to resolve it responsibly.

Using Absolutes

"I *never* get to play."

"He *always* gets to go."

"I'm the *only one* who doesn't get to watch that show."

"*Everyone else* does it."

Rarely are these statements true. Children can correct these statements by questioning their assumptions. When you hear an absolute statement, have your child restate it more specifically. Instead of saying, "*Everyone* does it," the child can learn to say *who specifically* does it. Using absolutes is overgeneralization and is actually a precursor to lying.

Using a Double Standard

Sometimes adults are guiltier of this flaw than children are. In fact, your child may have even noticed it in you. Yet children can be guilty as well, especially when it comes to their friends and siblings.

"Mom! Jacob won't put down my Game Boy."

"Are you going to play with it?"

"No, but he didn't ask if he could play with it."

"But you let Justin play with it when he was here."

"So?"

"Did Justin ask if he could play with it?"

"No, but he's my friend."

"So friends don't have to ask permission, but brothers do?"

This is an opportunity to talk about double standards. There are numerous teachable moments like this for you to take the time to teach the truth. Double-standard arguments are pointless. They permeate and separate relationships and workplaces. Children can learn now to ask themselves why they say what they say—before someone else does.

Shifting the Burden of Proof

Keep your ears open and you'll hear people shifting the burden of proof all around you. Have you ever heard these questions: "Why did *you* give me a *C*?" or "Why didn't *you* pick my son for the team?" This is a symptom of not being willing to take responsibility. Although courtroom dramas use this as a primary plot element, it doesn't teach children critical thinking. The truth is that students' grades are determined by their own effort and performance, and competitive sports are based on the player's ability and performance. Help your child to look in the mirror before pointing his finger elsewhere.

Irrational Appeal

Sometimes we substitute careful reasoning with irrational appeal. For example, we may say, "We mustn't change for is long established" (an appeal to tradition), or, "Things could go wrong" (an appeal to apprehension), or, "This might offend someone" (an appeal to a code of conduct). There's nothing wrong with using appeals, that is, until they appeal to emotions rather than minds. Emotion focuses on the feelings that ideas convey rather than the ideas themselves. Shifting the focus to the specific virtues of an idea can correct this. Rational appeal acts in conformity to reason.

Teach your children how to offer a rational appeal when appropriate. If you've asked them to do something or said no to one of their requests, they may appeal—if it includes additional information or a respectful request. But as the parent, you may choose not to hear their appeal, and they must learn to accept that as well.

"Kate, please vacuum the living room after you finish your homework."

"Yes, Mom."

A moment later: "Mom? May I appeal?"

"Yes, Kate."

"I promised Sue I'd call her after I finished my homework to give her the assignment. Can I wait to vacuum until after the phone call?"

"That's fine, Kate. Thanks for letting me know."

Kate barely sounds like a child. But she is. She just gave her mom the additional information in a way that was reasonable and respectful. Her mom could have chosen to deny her appeal, but she'd be hard-pressed to do so with such a respectful request. Look for opportunities to say yes to your children, and show them how to approach appeals in a rational way.

Critical Thinkers Utilize the Scientific Method

This age-old method of gathering and analyzing information is quite effective with children. Although flaws in the method do exist, its basic structure is useful for uncovering truth, especially if the incident in question was not witnessed firsthand. It also seeks to minimize the influence of bias or prejudice.

What kinds of problems can be solved with the scientific method? When one can isolate a problem or situation by eliminating extraneous factors, or when a system can be repeatedly tested through limited, controlled changes, the scientific method is very useful.

When utilizing the scientific method:

State the question.

Is there something you're wondering about? What problems are you currently facing in everyday life? This important step begins with determining the right question to ask: "Why isn't the telephone working?" "What is the quickest way to walk to school?" "Who is eating all the chocolate-chip cookies?" "How can I get my homework done more quickly?"

Form a hypothesis to explain it.

This will typically be the most plausible answer to the question that you can test. For the question, "What is the quickest way to walk to school?" your hypothesis might be, "Cross Maple Street, walk three blocks west, six blocks north, and then three blocks west." But there are other routes to test as well.

Test the hypothesis through experimentation.

After you have established the question and your hypothesis, it is time to test your answer. In the previous example, you might try a variety of routes at the same time of day and record the results. You would probably have to perform this experiment several times to be sure your results were accurate.

Draw conclusions.

The conclusions you draw from your experiment will answer your question. Which route was the quickest? Did it depend upon the weather, the timing of the traffic light, or how much energy you have to make the walk? Is your conclusion acceptable, or should you go back and form a new hypothesis and test again?

The scientific method is a great way to take the emotion out of a problem, helping you look at it objectively and honestly.

Critical Thinkers Use Deductive Reasoning

Drawing conclusions from what is known is called basic reasoning. In order to do so effectively, acquiring accurate information is important, but learning to analyze the facts is just as important. Usually around the fourth grade, a child's growing mind begins to recognize it has some new gears. Your child may begin to shift into deductive reasoning, connecting the facts he's learned and discovering new relationships among them. This is when he begins to think about *why* he asks *why*.

Logic requires applying the skill of deductive reasoning to look for patterns and sets of relationships. Logic allows us to ask the question, "Does that conclusion follow the facts as I know them?" It can be applied to every subject a child learns. However, formal logic training is something from which a child can still benefit. There are five common fallacies or errors in logical reasoning that your child should learn to recognize.

In their book *The Well-Trained Mind* Jessie Wise and Susan Wise Bauer use the story of Snow White to illustrate five fallacies.[3] Any one of these fallacies could have caused Snow White to allow the wicked witch— disguised as a peasant woman peddling apples—to trick her into eating a poisoned piece of fruit.

- *Anecdotal evidence fallacy*—using a personal experience to prove a point: *I've met peasant women before, and none of them ever poisoned me,* Snow White thinks to herself.
- *Argumentum ad hominem*—an attack on the speaker rather than on the argument itself. The peasant woman attacks the dwarves' motives: "Did the dwarves tell you not to let anyone in? They just want you to keep on cooking their meals and scrubbing their floors."
- *Argumentum ad misericordiam*—an appeal to pity: "I'm just a poor peasant woman trying to earn a penny for my sick children. You should let me in."

- *Argumentum ad verecundiam*—an appeal to authority. It may use the name of a famous person in support of an assertion: "I just sold an apple to the king, and he said it was the best apple he ever ate!"
- *Argumentum ad lazarum*—the assumption that a poor person is automatically more virtuous than a rich person: "I'm just a simple beggar woman, so I'd never hurt you."

If you take a close look at these fallacies, you begin to notice them everywhere. Political speeches, publicity campaigns, election slogans, newspaper editorials, even your child's textbooks often use faulty logic to mold people to a different point of view.

Logical thinking has three stages: the premise, the argument, and the conclusion.

In the first stage, there may be more than one premise. The key is to make sure that the first premise is true before drawing any conclusions based on it. The argument will determine the validity of the premise. A false premise will always yield a false conclusion:

Premise A: The earth is a flat surface.

Premise B: It is possible to fall off the edge of a flat surface.

Conclusion: It is possible to fall off the edge of the earth.

The false Premise A creates an incorrect conclusion.

Premise A: The magic mirror always tells the truth.

Premise B: The mirror says Snow White is more beautiful than I.

Conclusion: Snow White is more beautiful than I.

This conclusion is valid, based on the premise of the story.

Let's try to simplify the discussion for use with children. Replace the premises above with *if/then* statements.

If *the magic mirror always tells the truth,* and *the mirror says Snow White is more beautiful than I am,* then *Snow White is more beautiful than I am.*

If the first statement is true, and the logic is not faulty, the conclusion will always be accurate. Our children will make decisions, such as how to respond to peer pressure or which career path to choose, based on such deductive reasoning. Educate yourself in the language of logic to help lead them in uncovering the right conclusions.

Recognizing Truth

In this world where truth can be elusive, it is crucial for children to know how to recognize truth so they can judge accurately among the many false ideas that could lead them astray. *Discernment* is more than just a nice word—it could mean your child's very survival. This fact cannot be overemphasized! Discerning between hot and cold surfaces, safe and unsafe situations, a red light and a green light: In all of these cases, to *discern* means to be able to see and understand differences. *Discerning the truth* is being able to see and understand what is true—and what is not.

Discernment implies judgment. When we make assertions about truth or about how something was handled, we are required to make judgments. And these judgments are only as good as the evidence supporting them. If evidence is sketchy or not there, the judgment can bring with it untold harm. We see examples of poor judgment from insufficient evidence all the time. Because we are all human, our judgments can easily be flawed.

So how can we make sure our judgments are correct?

Gather sufficient evidence.

What helps you reach a conclusion or make a judgment? Evidence can include factual details, statistics, examples, cases in point, anecdotes, quotations, comparisons, descriptions, definitions, experience, unique knowledge, or any number of other things that can sufficiently remove reasonable doubt and establish *certainty*. It's not easy to establish certainty, so more often than not you will have to settle for *probability*.

Interpret evidence.

Does the evidence prove the majority or minority group to be right? If your daughter claims that "*everyone* she knows is going to the party," you can probably assume that is not true. Upon investigation, you may find that only her best friend is going, so that lack of evidence for your daughter's claim proves her argument insufficient. Evaluate all the available evidence before declaring it sufficient.

Avoid prejudice and blind faith.

We all hear and make statements that are full of prejudice or blind faith. Prejudice is an opinion or judgment conceived without proof or competent evidence. Blind faith is belief in something without factual or experiential evidence. Both assertions are based on ignorance. We must investigate what we believe to be true and teach our children to do the same.

Reconsider judgments in light of any new evidence.

When new evidence presents a challenge to a previous judgment, we must be willing to reconsider our deductions. Circumstances change and previous evidence may no longer be sufficient. Be open to reconsidering your judgment—if the new evidence is indeed sufficient.

Becoming a critical thinker will propel your child forward in the quest for success. His success at school and in his work will become "supercharged." His relationships will be sturdier. At times you may feel as though you are dragging reasons out of him, but the ability to reason is one of the chief signs of maturity. Young children are not developmentally capable of considering, evaluating, and offering reasons. Yet a child encouraged by his parents in these qualities can develop early abilities and gain a head start. Begin to encourage your child to offer reasons and not excuses.

Your Turn to Learn

One of the worst dispositions to have is double-mindedness. A person who is easily swayed by another doesn't possess the abilities for discerning truth. But we think based on what we discern to be true, and we act on what we think. Therefore, our beliefs are vitally important! Uncertainty is easily overcome by deception. Exercising discernment is necessary before we can learn to uncover truth, let alone teach a child to do so.

- Do you believe in the concept of absolute truth? Do you think there is a definitive answer to the question of whether or not something can be irrefutable? Upon what do you base your belief?
- Do you struggle to assert what you believe to be the truth? Do you worry about what others think of you when you do?
- Are you willing to systematically break down a problem instead of just react to it emotionally?
- Do you usually ask *why*, or do you find yourself accepting the reasons others give you?
- Are you active in looking for and presenting evidence to back up your opinions?
- Do you answer your child's questions of *why*, or do you commonly avoid or redirect them?

Connections

Every day children face opportunities to choose—right from wrong, to believe or not to believe, to obey or disobey. Unfortunately, peer pressure also begins early. Watch a toddler follow a child climbing on the "big toy" on the playground after his mom distinctly told him no. These tendencies must be addressed early in life, before junior-high school when the child is offered a cigarette.

For any truth to exist as truth, logically there must be an absolute truth, something that is always true no matter what. Whether or not something *feels* true is not the test for whether it is *absolutely* true or not. We all wrestle with peer pressure; we face it every day as others try to influence our beliefs and decisions. When you stand for truth, no matter the situation, you experience self-confidence. Rejection, isolation, even hostility from others should never be a reason for your child to disregard or reject the truths he has affirmed.

Teach your child to rely on absolute truth with these suggested exercises:

✔ Home

Exaggeration is a common trait among young children. Don't let it slide when you hear it coming out of your own child. Stop her and ask specifically to what she is referring. Are her facts accurate? Sometimes she may be bragging, other times she may simply be making an effort to feel included, but children can quickly become experts at the game of "one-upmanship." Use the opportunity to help her understand why she's trying to gain the approval of her friends. Then teach her about whose respect she should really be trying to gain.

> *Show & Tell*: If your child has difficulty in this area, there's a strong possibility you may be exaggerating as well. Monitor your own conversations with family, friends, and colleagues. If your child should happen to overhear you, use the occasion to guide him to being honest and forthright in his communication.

✔ School

As children advance to middle and high school, they will be continually confronted with conflicting opinions about right and wrong and the

standards of absolute truth. They need guidance about when and how they should stand on the truth. Help them now so that when they go off to college and have one of those 2 A.M. debates with a roommate, they will be able to offer an answer for why they believe what they believe.

Show & Tell: Once in a while read the editorial page aloud to your kids. Consider different opinions about a particular issue. You can offer yours as well, but make sure you give them a chance to state what they think and ask for the supporting evidence for their belief.

✔ Work

Problems abound and decisions have to be made in work situations. Your child's first job will introduce him to a host of problems he hasn't encountered before. What if he is wrongly accused of something? What if he has difficulty completing a certain task? Present some scenarios and help him think about how he can stay emotionally detached enough to identify certain problems and come up with logical solutions.

Show & Tell: We all want to leave our work at the office, but if we never share with our family how we face and deal with particular problems there, they might think we don't want them to talk about theirs. If you have faced a problem at work, let your family know how you solved it and ask for opinions on how they might have handled it themselves.

Family Activity

The Great Books Foundation strives to improve critical thinking skills through great literature. The "Junior Great Books" program is used in schools, enrichment classes, after-school clubs, and by homeschoolers.

Students learn how to ask questions about what they read—especially *why* questions. Below is an excerpt from the Parents' Corner on The Great Books Foundation's Web site. This is not as much an activity as it is a way of thinking to enrich the skills needed for critical thinking in all children, from toddlers to teens.[4]

Reading and Conversing at Home

While listening, talking, and playing, your young child develops important language pre-reading skills every day. Putting thoughts into words, acquiring new words to describe feelings and surroundings, and knowing that his or her thoughts and words are valued all help to build language skills. Here are suggestions for activities you can do with your toddler or preschooler to foster this very important developmental process.

The Art of Conversation

From infancy on, a child attempts to communicate, whether through talking or gestures. These need to elicit a response from you. When your child motions for an object, name that object and expand on it when possible: "Here's a cookie. A chocolate-chip cookie. A yummy chocolate-chip cookie."

Other ways to encourage conversation with your child might include:

- Letting your child's interest be a focus of conversation. When something captures your child's imagination, take the role of novice and let your child take the role of expert. Ask questions as long as your child enjoys answering them.
- Sharing family news during mealtimes. Ask specific questions that require more than a yes or no answer. For example, instead of asking, "Did you have fun at the playground today?" ask, "Who was at the playground with you today?" or, "What's your favorite thing to do at the playground?"

- Tolerating moments of silence. Children often need time to figure out what they want to say. If you jump in and fill the silences for them, they don't have the opportunity to put things into their own words.
- Turning off the TV. It's almost impossible to engage a young child in conversation when other stimuli are competing for his or her attention.
- Challenging your child to go beyond passive viewing when watching TV. Watch TV with your children and ask questions such as, "Why do you think that happened?" Such questions will help your child go beyond the immediate situation and begin to form connections that are crucial to their critical thought process.
- Allowing your child to speak with guests in your home. Your child will learn about introductions and greetings and also may gain a new perspective by hearing a different viewpoint.

The Joy of Reading

Reading to your child, no matter how young they are, is the first step in building a lifelong love of books. From following the direction of the words on the page, to turning the pages and beginning to match sounds with symbols, children naturally acquire reading-readiness skills as they listen to their favorite stories read to them again and again.

Here are some tips for reading with children:
- Keep the pace slightly slower than normal conversation and read with expression.
- Encourage your child to point things out about the book and ask questions.
- Pause from time to time to find out what your child thinks will happen next.

- Return to old favorites. Children love to hear the same stories again and again. As your child becomes more familiar with the vocabulary and events in the story, he or she will begin to associate certain spoken words with their corresponding spellings. This is referred to as building a "sight vocabulary."
- After completing the story, talk about the funniest, saddest, scariest, or most interesting part of the book.
- Model reading strategies for your child by sharing your reactions to the story and your questions about it. You may be surprised by the discussions such sharing sparks!

Chapter Six

An Information Manager

*"At the LORD's command Moses recorded
the stages in their journey."*
—NUMBERS 33:2

M om, can I call Toys 'R' Us to find out the price of a game?" Chris asked.

"Sure," I replied. "Do you know the number?" I was surprised and delighted at his initiative. Usually this was something I had to do *for* him.

"No, but I'll look it up in the phone book. No problem," he said with newfound confidence.

I watched as our nine-year-old son flipped through the yellow pages while mouthing the alphabet. His finger stopped when he found what he wanted, and a smile crept across his face. I walked away, but stayed within earshot. After he dialed the number, I heard him politely ask the store manager his question, thank him, and hang up the phone. Mission accomplished. A wave of pride swept over me.

"One down, one to go," I whispered to myself. His little brother would have help in acquiring this skill for himself.

Becoming confident in using a phone book, a dictionary, a card catalog, an encyclopedia, or the Internet doesn't happen overnight. But once your child knows where to go to find the information he needs, you'll rarely need to help him. All it takes is a little time to show him how he can feel completely at home with any sort of reference material.

These days, simply locating the right information has become a highly advanced skill. Much practice and experience is required before a child can successfully navigate the sea of information that is available today. Following that, *how* they deal with the information they find is of utmost importance. Adults face this problem as well: Someone may find an incredible fact that could change the lives of millions of people, but if they're unable to effectively *manage* that information, their vision could fade before they find the proper way to communicate it.

In managing information, the process is key.

During the years we homeschooled, my boys each did an independent research project on a subject of their choice. For my first grader it seemed like an overwhelming task. After he chose his subject (big cats such as lions and tigers), we went to the library and checked out a mountain of books and videos on the subject. Analyzing and interpreting the information was the next step. We examined one resource at a time and when we finished one, I asked him to tell me one interesting fact he learned from it. We wrote down each fact and by the time we were through, we had 20 facts about big cats. It was his first experience with paraphrasing information, and it was a huge success.

In order for a first grader to be able to communicate this information,

and for the other first graders to understand it (he was presenting to first graders at an elementary school), we decided he would need to stick to a simple book format. We considered making a display board, but decided that a report could be read aloud and then passed around for inspection by his classmates. We grouped all his facts by specific topics (types of cats, where they live, and what they eat) to create paragraphs. Then he pasted each section onto a sheet of paper to make up a first draft. After reading it aloud he found some statements he wanted to change. After he did so, I typed it for him and printed out his completed sheets for him to illustrate. We bound the eight pages together, and he designed a cover. In the end, it turned out beautifully, and my son could take legitimate pride in his accomplishment.

To become proficient information managers, children must be taught how to *acquire* information among many different sources, how to *analyze* the usefulness of the information to the topic, and how to *organize* the findings in the most accessible and efficient way. Finally, the ability to *synthesize* the information provides the ability to communicate the new or innovative idea behind the facts.

Information Managers Acquire Information

Knowing where to find the information is the first step. Knowing whom to ask for help is just as important. Yet in these busy lives we lead, there is often little time to search for all of the information that they need. Your job is to first teach your child how to employ the initiative he will need to find the answers himself. Successful information managers work for their answers rather than simply looking for handouts. The answers are out there, but children need to learn to find them on their own.

When it comes to where they get information, children (like adults) develop habits. In elementary school, on a special project, some children generally prefer print material to gather information from. Others prefer

using the Internet. Since most schools are connected to the Internet, these days children are encouraged to cite at least some of their information from an online source.

Colleges and universities expect incoming students to be proficient researchers. Yet because elementary and high schools don't always teach this skill, you should be sure that if no one else provides this instruction to your child, you do.

Growing up, I thought that acquiring a lot of different kinds of information meant using more than one brand of encyclopedia! Today, we have access to so much more information. Books, periodicals, newspapers, the Internet, CD-ROMs, and videos are all good sources for information your child can use to research a school report. And many different sources make for a more interesting and complete report.

Why is variety important? As a teacher and as an author I can tell you that relying on a variety of research helps to eliminate inconsistent or even incorrect information. When our youngest son was researching a town for his state history project, we discovered a person who was considered a significant figure in the town's historical records. Unfortunately, the person's name was spelled differently in the first two sources we found. Obviously, we had to do further research to find out which was the correct spelling. In our age of information, this happens more often than you'd expect. The facts are not always accurate, and the task falls to the researcher to find the most reliable data.

Another reason to use a variety of sources is that each author has his own point of view. It makes sense that different authors would have different perspectives and concentrate on different aspects of a topic. The use of different sources provides more perspectives, and a report or project of this kind presents a more balanced understanding.

Finding information from a variety of sources is like fishing with a net. When you throw your net into the water and pull it back onto the boat, it may be teeming with different types of fish. However, if you're fishing for tuna, you'll have to pick through your catch, find what you want, and throw the rest back. In the same way, one resource may have many different types of information. Once you've recovered a healthy catch, then it's a matter of deciding whether or not what you found is what you need.

When our oldest son, Christopher, began to work on his first science-fair project in sixth grade, he needed to find information about citrus fruit and electricity. His question was, "Which citrus fruit generates the most electricity?" In order to understand how and why fruit do this in the first place, he needed to do some research. When I say "do some research," I am really saying "go find out as much as possible on this topic and bring back only the relevant findings." So Christopher did.

He began with an Internet search using the keywords *fruit* and *electricity*. He searched using many different words, including *science-fair projects*. Then he went to the library and did the same thing in the online card catalog. After a week of research he had a mountain of data, books, magazine articles, and even some actual scientific studies. It was overwhelming to look at it all! His next job would be to sift through and evaluate whether or not any of it was what he needed.

Information Managers Analyze Information

This is something we do every day—at home and in our jobs. It happens as commonly as when we seek out the perfect gift for someone we love. Using our knowledge of that person's interests and tastes, we know right away whether or not a particular item is suitable for our mom, dad, sister, or spouse. We evaluate each choice for its appropriateness and relevance. And when it comes down to the final decision, a tie between two items might lead to a deeper analysis of each of their unique features to determine the perfect choice.

Does your child know how to paraphrase information? Does he have the skills to communicate that information in writing or orally in a way that is easily understood? Sometimes the information we gather must then be communicated to a third party. Our children need to learn how to do that in a succinct way if it is to be understood.

We homeschooled our boys for four years and during that time I had the opportunity to work on this aspect of their education. Back when I was in school and assigned a report, I had no real understanding about how to present that information back to my teacher. It was a hit-and-miss situation. Even though it took me until college before I effectively learned to summarize, paraphrase, and synthesize information, I know that a first grader can learn how because mine did!

When you evaluate something, you appraise its value. Are its attributes relevant to your search? Why did it attract you? Does it fill a need or answer a question you have? Consider why it appeals to you. We'll discuss this more in the section on synthesizing.

Information Managers Record Information

Some teachers encourage note-taking as early as first grade. Unfortunately, there isn't much consistency among teachers in this area. Some teach it, some do not. And so some children never become adept at writing down what's pertinent in the teacher's discussion. But by the time children reach middle school, note-taking is usually expected.

This was one area in which our oldest son was not proficient when he moved from homeschooling to a public middle school in the sixth grade. He had a hard time deciding what was important to write down from the lesson and what wasn't. Then what he did write down wasn't always legible! It took a concerted effort on our part to help him gain this important skill, but by the end of the school year, he was able to take notes somewhat successfully. He still hadn't completely mastered the skill, but he had shown marked improvement.

A companion skill to note-taking is identifying the main idea in a paragraph or passage. This skill helps children become better at discerning what's important and what isn't. You can practice this skill at home using something you are already reading with them or with stories from the newspaper. In fact, newspapers offer a wonderful opportunity to practice picking out important facts.

As our children learn how to make judgments about what they read, they will also become more discerning about what they hear. Most teachers will employ and support this skill, but parents can help tremendously as well. If your child isn't already learning this skill in school, there are many ways to teach it. If your child is a first or second grader, you might watch a video and ask her to help you write down one thing she learned from it. If she is older, you might give her several resources and have her come up with an accompanying reflection or paragraph about what she learned from each source.

Sometimes my children come home from the library with a mountain of books to use for an assignment. If each source were actually used, it would become a cumbersome task to keep track of each piece of information. Children can easily become overwhelmed and may decide they don't even want to try. It's up to us to help them break the assignment down into small steps.

One way to make this easier is to use sticky notes. Use small ones to mark single facts in a book, and larger ones to mark sections of pertinent information. Go through each resource this way and after finding the relevant information in each, have your child write down the title, the author, the page number, and any other required information for the bibliography.

A bibliography becomes a requirement in the later elementary years, but a child is never too young to learn how to develop one. Not only is it

important in showing the variety of sources used, it also gives credit to the authors who originally provided the facts used in the paper.[1] Besides these more obvious reasons, children need to learn early on that they can not take credit for things they did not come up with on their own.

Information Managers Organize Information

William Blake once said, "I must create a system, or be enslaved by another man's."[2] How does your child organize his information? Has he created a system for managing it, or does it end up in various places throughout the house? Maybe the first question to ask should be, "Where should the information be kept?"

Do you have trouble keeping track of important phone numbers or addresses? Maybe you can't find all the vacation information you collected for that anniversary cruise you wanted to take. Or maybe you contacted the same insurance company three times for a quote because you misplaced the previous information! You might be good at gathering and evaluating information, but maintaining it is also essential to the process.

In order to manage information efficiently, we need a system. Yet even before that, we need to address just how orderly we really are and in what areas we could use some work. In our world, order is the rule of the day, from skyscrapers to ecosystems—without order we would have chaos. A system for keeping track of information helps to keep our own personal chaos at bay. (By the way, I define *chaos* a little differently than the philosophers: In my house, chaos is called the *Can't-Have-Anyone-Over Syndrome!*)

From library books to be returned to school papers that disappear into the "black hole" in the backpack, there are many things that children need to learn to manage, and do so in a way that is logical to them. But first you as the parent must make it a priority. There are many practical ways to encourage this, but all require commitment.

When my son began to research his science-fair project, he did a great job gathering and evaluating the information. Unfortunately, I discovered that he had a penchant for leaving this information all over his desk, on the floor, under his bed, in his already-overcrowded backpack, in his locker, and peeking out from between the wall and the computer table. He may have found the information once, but would he ever find it again? Probably not! How does one manage such a mess?

Here are a few ideas:

File Folders

This is the most economical way to store paperwork of any kind. When your child announces he has to do a report or project of some kind, take out a file folder, write the name of the project on the tab, and give it to him. Keep in mind that giving it to him may not be enough. Even though you would assume a file folder is relatively easy to use, I find paper on top of it, under it, and around it more often than I find paper in it! So explain that every piece of paper that has to do with this project belongs in the folder. You may have to use multiple folders for a large project. Keep them labeled, and keep them together.

Computers

Every student can benefit from learning to use a computer. Even if your child prefers to write out his information, he still needs to gain adequate skills in accessing and printing it. Can he save it as a file and then find it again when changes are made? Can he print and change the printing options to create the best possible final product? If computers only serve as glorified video games, you are missing a huge opportunity. Many schools have computer labs, and although they aren't the most efficient place to learn these skills, it's still a place to start. But if your school does not offer the opportunity, that doesn't mean you have to wait. There are software

programs available that teach typing and competence in specific computer programs and applications, some designed for children as young as kindergarten! Learning how to type takes consistent practice, but 10 minutes a day as part of a daily routine can have children typing in no time. Using computer disks to store information, learning about file formats, accessing the information, and printing from a disk are also useful skills. Yet it's good to remind children to be careful not to over-decorate their papers—the information is not made more or less complete by cluttering up the page! Remember, the goal is to produce a quality product that enhances the presentation of the information. And if your child is able to use the Internet to research papers, he can save interesting files or graphics to a disk for later use, cutting down on all that paper he has to manage in his file folders.

Shelving and Storage

Every child should have space for her books and reading materials. Reference books like encyclopedias, dictionaries, and science and history books all need to be easily accessible and preferably in one place. With the advent of CD-ROMs and Internet resources, things like atlases and encyclopedias have become digitized for even more convenience. Soon, we are told, there won't be any need for bookshelves at all! Think what you will, but I believe we will always have a love of "old-fashioned" books, "hardcopy" magazines, and "touchable" reference guides. All these things need their own well-maintained and orderly place in the home.

Where does your child currently keep notebook paper, extra pencils and pens, and project materials like a stapler, hole-punch, or glue? You can make it easier by keeping all these things in one place and encouraging children to help maintain these things in their proper place. You could keep everything in cupboards or drawers, but sometimes a bucket, basket, or bin is better for managing bulky school supplies, materials, tools, and

even those ultra-organized file folders you just put together. The best thing about the buckets is their portability: Your child can just take their stuff with them when they're off to work on that science-fair project.

Information Managers Synthesize Information

Graduate school was an awakening for me. The intense reading, research, and reporting required me to find volumes of information among an astonishing variety of sources and then summarize the content. Yet it was in synthesizing the information that I found the most trouble. I knew how to form a *thesis*. I knew how to *analyze* and *evaluate* it. But *synthesis* was entirely new. When I finally learned to synthesize, it was as if a new world was opened to me. The possibilities exploded. My dreams seemed available to materialize into reality. The most learned and well-respected theories could now be called into question if I so desired.

It might be said that learning to synthesize information is one of the talents most responsible for designating genius. And whether we are in a graduate program or still in kindergarten, being able to synthesize is how we see what is new in what is old; it is the creative aspect of acuity most responsible for successful information management.

Synthesis means the combination of diverse parts or elements into a complex whole. Once all the information is gathered, categorized, and summarized, what does it say? What do you see that wasn't there before? What's the bottom line? In school, children learn how to write topic paragraphs. But writing conclusions is usually the last thing they learn. There are formulas to writing and most schools work hard to teach theirs. But many of them are missing the point, which is, *What is this information telling you? What new thing can you learn from all of this?*

When I was asked to judge a fourth-grade writing contest sponsored by Barnes & Noble, I read 120 entries. My goal was to come up with three winners, and not surprisingly, it wasn't easy. Unfortunately, it wasn't because they were all so good; I couldn't find three that deserved to win.

Technically, the students were excellent writers. They had their writing formulas down. But the heart in the information they were presenting, that spark of passion that showed true interest was completely absent. They were dry and static, almost as if the kids were being punished or forced to participate.

One of things I wanted to tell them was to include *their own opinion* about what they had researched and reported on. We all want to know how the information applies to us and what we can take away from the experience. But what causes us to jump up and down, to get excited, and remember what we read weeks, months, or even years after we've read it? What did the writer learn in the course of researching that changed her mind and will change mine too?

Even elementary school teachers can read a student's writing and have their minds changed on a certain subject as a result. I remember an essay from a sixth grader who told the story of the buffalo from the Native American's point of view. I was absolutely riveted and by the end, I was deeply moved. That little paper changed a significant piece of American history for me. Your child can do the same for his teacher.

Becoming an information manager is like being a detective and uncovering the truth about a supposed crime. Your task is to explain how this information could have fallen by the wayside. You hunt for the unusual, the surprising, and the more interesting facts, gathering information and immersing yourself in the case until you know it forward and backward. And when the time finally comes to communicate your findings to the world, they are not shaken by questions or disagreements. The questions become invitations to spread your newfound passion.

Possibly more than any other skill, becoming an information manager can produce incredible results. It is a skill that expands our mental borders

and teaches us to see that unique territory a little more clearly, a little more broadly. Once your child learns to manage information, it's a small step from there to discovering those places his imagination will never tire of exploring.

—⁓— Your Turn to Learn

Are you frequently tempted to throw everything into the "circular file" instead of trying to manage all the information that comes into your home? Obtaining useful information is one skill, organizing it is another. If you don't have an information system (or could use some encouragement in maintaining it), you may want to ask yourself some of the following questions before helping your child with his.

- Are your paper files easy to find and access? Do you frequently sift through the papers and keep only what you really need?
- Do you have a system for paying bills?
- Do you use a calendar to keep track of events and activities?
- Does your information-management system include subcategories for organizing particular tasks like where to keep coupons for grocery shopping or decorating ideas for the baby's room?
- What happens to the old magazines in your house? Do you keep all those catalogs? What about school papers brought home?
- When you are planning to purchase a big-ticket item, such as a car or a refrigerator, where do you store your research?
- Do you consider alternative systems if a more convenient idea presents itself?

Connections

We must all learn to organize information and present it accurately in a way that is convenient for the recipient. Try some of these suggestions for encouraging this important trait in your child.

✔ Home

Planning a party requires a number of pieces of information to be organized and communicated. Where will the party be held? Will there be a cost? If so, how much will it be per person? How many friends can you afford to invite? How long will the party last? What decorations and activities will you provide? How much will those things cost? How will you make the invitations? How will you keep track of RSVPs?

Show & Tell: If your child is not old enough yet to plan his own party, let him see the entire process as you go through it with him.

✔ School

If your child decided to run for student council, what might be required to get his name on the ballot? What would his message be to his fellow students? What would be the best way to get that message out? What about flyers and posters?

Show & Tell: Are you a member of the PTA or some other committee? Where do you keep all the paperwork related to that committee? How do you communicate with other members? How do you communicate with those outside the committee?

✔ Work

What does your child want to be when she grows up? Maybe she wants to be a veterinarian, but does she know what the job entails? Does she know what kind of schooling is required or how long it will take? Does she realize there are different types of veterinarians? And how do you start to sift through all the options? How do you evaluate whether a particular job fits your experience and the desires and needs of your family? Help your child begin to work through this process—and don't be discouraged if she eventually changes her mind!

Show & Tell: The tax man cometh! Even if your child isn't inter-ested in becoming a certified public accountant, someday he will be forced to file taxes. Organizing tax information and presenting it accurately is a process your child can learn and even enjoy if he's inclined to working with numbers. Itemizing deductions is a great opportunity to show the need for serious information-management skills.

Family Activity

Managing information doesn't have to be limited to paperwork. Family photos and memorabilia can be organized and presented in a chronological and visually pleasing way. If you've never made a scrapbook for your family, now's a good chance to involve your children in the process. You can even let them start their own and help them transfer their ideas onto the pages.

Managing our family information communicates that our memories are important to remember. For information on scrapbooking, visit the Creative Memories Web site at www.creativememories.com.

Chapter Seven

A Cooperative Learner

"God opposes the proud but gives grace to the humble."
—JAMES 4:6

There were eight 12-year-old boys in my house for Christopher's birthday party. It had disaster written all over it. Christopher planned to teach them a role-playing game so he was busy directing the teams, explaining the rules, and setting up the game. One of the boys had never played the game before and seemed apprehensive about the whole idea. Christopher put that boy on his team so he could be coached through the first round. Once the game got underway, my son became all things to all people—he was instructor, director, encourager, competitor, moderator, and friend. I'd had my doubts, but the party was a surprising success!

During the same month Christopher was involved in a group project for a science contest. There were three students in the group, and Christopher had assumed the role of leader. However, after eight weeks of working together the project was nowhere near completion. With the deadline only two weeks away, Christopher was still unable to get the other members to do their part. He ended up shouldering the burden of the entire project alone.

I asked him some reflective questions following the disappointment and frustration to figure out what went wrong. I discovered that he hadn't communicated his expectations very well to the group members. He hadn't encouraged their input, and they hadn't participated in the planning. Together, we realized that in some situations, cooperation is more valued than leadership.

Sometimes it's hard for our children to determine when they should lead and when they should follow. It takes practice. Teachers can try to foster leadership in certain situations, but their input is rarely enough to create lifelong habits. A family can offer many more opportunities to work cooperatively. That is, by definition, what a family is all about. For a child to be a true leader, he must know how to work with people. The following areas of focus will help you foster the skills that your child needs to be successful in cooperative situations as an adult.

Cooperative Learners Participate

While some children don't enjoy participating in a group, others have no trouble. Some children even seem to take control of every group they join. If your child is a natural-born leader, encourage him to participate in an activity that he *can't* lead, like Little League or piano lessons. As he gets older, encourage him to run for the student council or start a club at school. He might even head up a unique fundraiser or community service project.

Come up with projects you can do together that enlist the help of everyone in the family. Is there a ministry in which you can serve as a family? Maybe you could help the homeless or even tackle an environmental project such as cleaning up a trail or picking up trash in a park.

Everyone needs to learn to be a member of a group, as a family, and a team.

In her book *The Family Virtues Guide*, Linda Kavelin Popov describes 53 virtues for families to encourage. I've adapted a few here to address the needs of the cooperative learner; from these, three primary aspects can be ascertained to communicate to your child. Each can be encouraged on a daily basis with very little effort.

Purposefulness starts with the question, "What is it you are trying to accomplish?" But even before that, *proper* purposefulness requires considering the question, "*To whom* is this purpose really important?" Plenty of people start with the right motives but as they work, forget to continually check their progress. If your motives aren't honest or you can't remain focused on the proper purposes, your participation will be counterproductive. Distractions will always come along, and children especially will have to work hard to resist them. Staying on track requires keeping the goal in sight. It's as important with an individual goal as it is with a group goal. And as a member of a group, people count on you to be purposeful toward the group's motivation. Proper personal motives aren't enough; when someone in the group isn't clear about the purpose, they can become confused and aimless, and set everyone up for failure.

Reliability shows others that we can be depended on. They don't have to wonder if we will actually get it done. They know we will do what was agreed on, without forgetting or even having to be reminded. It is a highly valued quality, and one that some people never acquire. When children agree to work with a group to accomplish a specific goal, they must realize that they are being relied upon to keep that commitment. We all want to work with people who care about doing what they said they would, so that we can relax knowing the task is in capable hands. People who are all talk and no action, who seem to disappoint over and over, don't stick around long. Being reliable means doing the things we've promised to do, even if we're not in the mood.

Respectfulness is honoring the rules and individuals of the group, which in turn makes life more peaceful and orderly for all. Valuing others' opinions and responding to them kindly and without interruption are signs of respect. First, having respect for authority is crucial for children when they are learning to respect a group. Classrooms can become extensions of a child's family situation when a student's lack of respect is carried over from the home. And lack of respect by just one person will often ruin the unity of the entire group.

Do you model these qualities in your home with your children? Are you proactive in developing a common purpose and understanding, or do you simply react to your child's disrespect and unreliability? Are you reliable and responsible? Do you show your child respect for those around you, or do you act out of your own feelings and motives?

Cooperative Learners Serve

You can start cultivating an atmosphere in your family that says, "This is our family, and we all take care of it." Find ways to teach your children to serve one another, whether by serving soup to a sick sibling or offering to do chores for a brother or sister who has a lot of homework that night. The willingness to serve is essential to the success of any group, including the family. Otherwise, the goals of the group will never be met. Three qualities are necessary for true service to exist: caring, excellence, and helpfulness.

Linda Popov says, "*Caring* is giving love and attention to people and things that matter to you. You can show you care about someone by saying and doing things that help them. Caring about something you are doing means giving it your best."[1] Even as I watch my children weed their grandparents' garden, I see that they are motivated to do a good job for them because they care about them. (And then I wonder why they don't care as much about weeding our own garden!) When I think of myself as part of a family group, I am motivated to contribute to the well-being of that group. When we care, we show it by serving one another, taking the interests of others as our own. If we don't care, people will realize our selfish motivations and not care about us in return.

Excellence is a feature that describes how well we do what we do. As we learned in our discussion about quality in chapter two, the striving for excellence is one requirement to achieve quality. When serving a group, we should strive to do so with excellence. Most of us are all too familiar with the disappointment and frustration we experience when someone else does not strive for excellence. Let us teach our children to ensure they never cause those feelings in someone else.

Finally, *helpfulness* is a quality of service that arises from caring. Being helpful is assisting someone in something they need done. Maybe they can't do it themselves or don't have the time to do it. The key is in pleasing others rather than oneself. There are many times my husband will do something for me because he knows I can't or just don't have time. He may not like doing it, but he does it because he cares for me. Every morning he puts a load of laundry in the washer. He knows our busy lives are such that I have little time to get everything done. Five minutes of his time before he goes to work is a tremendous help to our family. It takes many hands to get things done in an efficiently operating group. But when we help other group members above and beyond our required service, it shows we care, makes that person's life a little easier, and gives them a great gift.

Service begins at home. What you cultivate in your family will extend to the world outside. My mother-in-law did a wonderful job cultivating a spirit of service in her sons, and for that I am eternally grateful. Hopefully, my future daughters-in-law will feel the same toward me someday.

Cooperative Learners Negotiate Toward Agreement

Teaching your child how to appeal a decision is great experience to help her negotiate in a group. She must be able to offer new information and communicate her request in a respectful manner. And in order to get her point across, she will need to learn to take into account the needs and preferences of others. Three qualities generally contribute to successful negotiations: assertiveness, consideration, and flexibility.

When you are *assertive*, you move forward with confidence in your decision or opinion. Peer pressure doesn't end when we graduate from high school. In our jobs, in our churches, and even in our families we need to be assertive, but not aggressive, about our own ideas and opinions. In a group situation you have to be willing to let others know what you will and will not do. When you negotiate, you must be willing to speak up for what you know is right.

There's a difference between being assertive and being aggressive. An aggressive person will try to control others, push them around, or even hurt them in order to get his own way. An assertive person remembers how worthy they are and stands up for the truth. They think for themselves and are not easily swayed. They ask for what they want or need. They freely express their thoughts and feelings about a particular issue.

Consideration is the other side of the same coin. When you are considerate, you have regard for other people and their feelings. That doesn't mean that you are swept away by their feelings when you make a decision, but it does help create balance during times of negotiation. Just as you think for yourself and stand for what you believe, others do the same. It is important that you give the same value to the ideas and opinions of others.

Negotiation is difficult in group situations when people don't practice consideration. Husbands and wives get a lot of practice in this skill. During arguments, assertiveness balanced with consideration should be the rule, but for some of us, this is a challenge. I come from a New York Sicilian family that has no difficulty voicing opinions assertively. However, consideration of the other's feelings tends to get overlooked. There is a balance to be reached between pressing your opinion and running over people. Family life offers daily practice of this quality!

Finally, there is the quality of *flexibility*. Whenever we work with any group of individuals, there is bound to be diversity, because no two people are alike. Because of this, we need to be flexible in our thinking. If you're flexible, you are open to new ideas and opinions. If you're flexible, you're willing to change your mind. Could this ever involve a compromise? Of course it could. But it shouldn't be a win-lose situation; it should be a win-win situation. For example, I bend to my husband's sense of order in our home. "Everything has a place," he says, "and everything should be in its place!" But he bends to my desire to have my own space in which I can be as neat (or as messy) as I want to be. Admittedly, flexibility of thought increases the same way that flexibility in our muscles increases—with practice and consistency.

The "Serenity Prayer" (commonly attributed to Reinhold Neibuhr) states: "God, grant me the serenity to accept the things I cannot change, courage to change the things I can, and the wisdom to know the difference." Flexibility is a skill we may learn late in life (I didn't learn it until after I was married), but those who have acquired it know that it allows for more joy in the journey!

Cooperative Learners Teach

Although some of us have the gift of teaching, it is a skill that can be learned by anyone. Older children don't always have a lot of *patience* for younger siblings or classmates who don't catch on as quickly as they do. So when teaching a new skill, you must also teach *compassion* for others and *respect* for each other's gifts.

My husband readily admits he isn't a good teacher; he doesn't have the patience. But he has been able to develop his skill with practice and a conscious effort on his part. Popov says, "Patience means waiting. It is enduring a delay or troublesome situation without complaining."[2] When we work together in groups, there will inevitably be delays. People won't understand right away what you are trying to teach them. They will do it wrong or not at all. Group dynamics can be fragile and a lack of patience will hasten it to its end.

Showing compassion for those we are teaching lets them know we care. Everyone makes mistakes, and that can make us feel like an outsider. Popov explains, "Being compassionate tells a person that they are not alone. It makes you a friend when someone needs a friend. It gives you a good feeling and makes you useful at the same time."[3]

At one point, Charles was having a great deal of difficulty completing his times tables within the given time frame. He was frustrated and didn't want to try anymore. His older brother, Christopher, noticed his frustration and encouraged him to try again. This time Charles completed five more than before. When Christopher congratulated him on his progress, Charles's countenance changed completely. He started trying harder even though he still had a long way to go. Imagine what that show of compassion from his brother meant to him.

A good way to model respect for others' gifts is by complimenting others in front of your child. Everyone has been given gifts and taking the time to recognize those is a critical skill for success. Sometimes groups don't work because we aren't noticing everyone's true talents. Compliments can go a long way to encouraging these and keeping the group running.

Another way to encourage this respect is to work together on tasks where you can assign jobs based upon people's gifts. A garage sale or community yard sale is a great opportunity for this. Artistic children who pay

attention to detail can make great signs. Organizers and number crunchers are natural cashiers. Gregarious and personable children can greet potential buyers with their happy faces.

Cooperative Learners Work with Group Dynamics

You don't have to travel abroad to appreciate cultural differences. You can experience them just driving from New York to Florida! But within our own neighborhoods, schools, and churches we know people who both believe and behave differently from us. Keep in mind the customs and language of the group with which you are working.

Children will learn that there are some people they cannot please or convince to their way of thinking. So we must practice the qualities of working within group dynamics every day in our homes, in our schools, and on the job—the qualities of unity, tact, and appreciation. We can guide our younger children on how to interact successfully, so that when they are older, they will have what they need to "get along."

Unity brings harmony and peace. When working with others, a sense of unity is crucial to meet the needs of others. Unity means you value what *each* person brings to the group, and you don't try to make everyone else do things your way. It is more than just consideration; it means finding common ground between you and other people. And the most basic of commonalities among humans is that God has created us all. It is not a mistake that we are all different. It is by design.

Without a sense of unity, people have an us-against-them mentality. In families that mentality comes out in sibling rivalry or parental preference. Disunity can be seen between different political parties, races, religions, levels of income, and even between husbands and wives. It is probably our world's greatest struggle—the struggle for unity. As we work together in groups we must find a common ground, whether it is a goal or a project

or an ideal. Then we can recognize the multitude of gifts in others and use them together for that specific purpose or goal.

Often when we are working with diverse individuals, *tact* is especially important. We may think we need to "speak the truth," but we should first think before we speak. Sometimes silence is the better choice. In today's society we are probably overly conscious of offending other people. In other words, we either lie or sit quietly while others are rude and demanding so as not to offend them. Being tactful means that you tell the truth, but you're kind when you do it. We all need feedback in our jobs and in our relationships, so learning how to give and accept constructive criticism is essential to working with others cooperatively.

We are all different. There are probably many things you'd like to change about someone else, but instead you need to learn *appreciation* for others' points of view. I know there are things I'd like to change about Chip, and I'm sure there are things he'd like to change about me. Yet when we appreciate the fact that we're different, we are flexible, and we accept what we cannot change with grace. A person who does not appreciate someone else's point of view will push for his own way and does not work well with other people. A complaining person breaks the unity of a group. I have seen many instances when one teacher broke the unity of an entire faculty because she didn't appreciate the different viewpoints of the other teachers. Sides were taken and lines were drawn. Wars can be started over a simple lack of appreciation. Shouldn't we raise children who will unify people instead?

Becoming a cooperative learner will take a great deal of practice. It does not come easily because by nature we are selfish beings, wanting our own way. Our families are the training ground for cooperation. We only have a few short years in which to impart this crucial component to a successful life into our children. Even though this world is a competitive place, cooperation drives us forward together and not alone.

✏ Your Turn to Learn

Learning how to work cooperatively toward a common goal is a foundational skill. In a family, we must work with the needs of others in mind. Some of us tend to control everything we can, while others shirk responsibility every chance they get. Where do you stand as a cooperative worker when you contemplate leading your child in this quality?

- Do you do your share of the group's duties?
- Do you push to have things done your way? (Be honest!)
- Do you listen to other people's ideas before making a decision?
- Do you accept the blame when things go wrong?
- Are you attentive to the opinions, desires, and interests of others?
- Do you encourage others in word and deed?
- Do you keep your promises?

Connections

The ability to get along with others, whether at home, in school, or on the job, is absolutely critical. We all notice when it's there, as well as when it isn't. A child who consistently fights with others on the playground or has a problem with sibling rivalry may be the son of a colleague whose annual evaluations on the job come back, "Needs improvement in social skills."

We would do well to remember that we are all in relationship with others, both learning from them and teaching them every day.

✔ Home

Cooperation begins with respect. At home you teach your children respect for authority, for property, and for others. Where else do they learn about respect?

Show & Tell: Respect is something one can see, but also can hear. How do you speak to your family members? How do you speak to others? On the road? On the phone? How do you speak to your in-laws? What does how you speak teach your children about respect?

✔ School

Your child has many chances to be the leader of a group. When your child's class has a substitute teacher, how does your child behave? Does he go along with the rowdiness of other children, or is he cooperative and helpful with the substitute?

Show & Tell: Are you cooperative with your child's school? Do you work with his teacher or against her? Do you contribute to group processes such as the PTA or other parent support groups? When your child sees you working with his school, what does he see? You must be his advocate without being someone else's adversary.

✔ Work

Today's companies utilize team-building strategies because they have been shown to lead to higher productivity and a more pleasant work environment. Since even McDonalds employs team-building strategies, there's a good chance your son or daughter will experience them at some point. Encourage him or her to participate fully in such activities and take advantage of the opportunity to cooperate.

Show & Tell: Do you have difficulty working with certain colleagues? Have your children heard about it? Do you make an effort to get along and engage your child in how you handle difficult situations?

Family Activity

A willingness to help others, even when you don't feel like it, is a crucial component to cooperation. We should be willing to help others, not for a reward, but because we are all members of the same group with the same goals. For the purpose of this activity, consider yourselves to be members of the same family. Using the questions below, encourage each other to look for opportunities to give someone else a hand.[4]

- When was the last time you needed help with something (carrying something, understanding something, going somewhere, etc.)?
- How did you feel when someone helped you?
- What are some ways that you can help someone out, either at school, at home, or in the community?
- If you are able to help someone, and do help him or her, how do you think the other person might feel toward you?
- If you knew that someone wouldn't even say "thanks" if you helped him or her, would you help him or her anyway?
- Have you ever forgotten to thank someone who helped you? Talk about it.
- How do you think you would feel about someone who was helpful even if they didn't want a reward? Would you admire them?

Chapter Eight

An Effective Communicator

"The wise in heart will be called understanding,
And sweetness of speech increases persuasiveness."
—PROVERBS 16:21 (NASB)

"Jessica, please tell your brother to put his dirty clothes in the laundry basket before he washes up for dinner," says Mom.

Jessica trudges off to find her brother.

"And do it *nicely,* please," Mom adds.

"James, Mom said to do the laundry before you come to dinner."

James looks up. "Why do I have to do the laundry? I've never done it before," he says incredulously.

"I don't know. That's what Mom said."

Later, everyone is at the dinner table waiting for James.

"Where is your brother?"

"I don't know."

Meanwhile, the smell of dinner wafts down the hall to the laundry room. "Forget it!" James throws down the detergent and runs to the kitchen, mouth watering.

"How long does it take to pick up your dirty clothes?" Mom asks when he finally arrives.

"I was doing the laundry," James replies.

Mom stares at him, dumbfounded. When James reaches for the rolls, Mom stops him mid-reach.

"Did you wash your hands?"

Figuring he's being singled out for abuse, James storms off to wash his hands and stays in a defensive mood for the rest of the evening.

Remember the telephone game? You tell one person a statement or a story, and each person keeps telling it to the next in line until it reaches the last person, who tells the story to the group as they understand it. Usually it comes out sounding totally different from what the first person had said! Why does this happen? Even though most of us have the best of intentions, the message still becomes a tangled mess. How often does this situation occur in your own family?

So many things depend on effective communication. Poor communication skills is the primary cause of many failed marriages. Everyone suffers when the communication is faulty. So how can we learn to communicate our thoughts, feelings, and opinions clearly?

What Is Effective Communication?

Every speaker knows when he's lost his audience—he can hear it in the silences. How effectively you communicate can be measured by audience attention, audience participation, and audience response. This is especially true between two people. When you speak to your children, you know whether or not they are listening and are actually hearing what you say.

Many speakers make the mistake of assuming that what they have to say is so important that everyone will listen to it. This is rarely true. And parents must do more than just assume that their message is getting across.

If you know your audience, you can often anticipate their reaction. Sometimes an audience will react negatively to what we communicate no matter how effectively we present it. However, a spoken message that gets missed or dismissed is usually the fault of a single person—the speaker— either because of inadequate preparation or a flawed delivery. Considering your technique as a communicator is wise before beginning to blame your audience.

This problem happens quite often in families—no more disastrously than between husband and wife. We all know how easily things can get misconstrued when we aren't willing to give up personal ground. So often with our children, we expect them to know the underlying meaning in what we say. But the old adage is helpful to remember: "Say what you mean, and mean what you say!" Our children depend on clear and effective communication from us, and again, it's a skill we first need to acquire ourselves before we can pass it on to our kids.

Even in our information-rich society, ineffective communication is commonplace. It is seen every day, everywhere. Teachers miscommunicate to students; children miscommunicate with their friends. Families, neighbors, church members all miscommunicate, with varied and unintended consequences.

My son's middle school took extensive measures to communicate to students that they should come to a teacher or staff member if they were experiencing trouble with another student. Yet when arguments between students erupted, the students still weren't coming to the teachers, and the administration couldn't understand why. They responded, "Well, we told them to come to us if they had a problem. We have done all we could do." They may have felt their communication was effective, but they never

checked to be certain that the message was received, understood, *and appreciated.* In this case, calling an assembly and making an announcement did not equate effective communication because the students did not appreciate the message.

When we communicate with our children, we have to do more than talk *at* them. Each child receives communication and interprets it differently. If our youngest doesn't respond verbally to what we say, we can be sure he hasn't understood. We all need to communicate in the most effective way for our audience.

On a scale of one to ten, how would you rate your effectiveness as a communicator? By putting some simple skills into practice, we could all improve in this area.

Tone vs. Content

Parents are famous for saying, "Watch your tone with me." Why? Because our tone communicates our true message. We all know that the words we say are rarely as important as how we say them. The message can easily be drowned out by our tone.

Tone begins rearing its ugly head in children around the age of three. Its companions can include such gestures as rolling eyes, hands on the hips, foot stomping, a stuck-out chin, gritted teeth, or crossed arms. Those of you with a child this age have surely seen this behavior. Skill in using tone develops with age, so setting standards for respectful behavior early is very important in a child's life. If a child speaks to authority in a tone that's less than respectful, and his behavior is excused, the issue is being avoided. It may be called "age-appropriate behavior," but it is never *appropriate.*

Many parents don't like hearing it, but a disrespectful tone is a learned behavior. Fortunately, since it's learned, it can be unlearned. Have you ever heard yourself in your child? I have to admit that when I hear our boys arguing, it's my own words and tone I hear coming out of them. If I want them to be respectful to one another, I have to first monitor my own level of respect. Children listen when we speak to others. They hear us on the phone. They overhear our conversations about teachers, friends, and in-laws. What do they hear when they listen? That should be a humbling thought!

You may not be able to control what your child hears at school or with her friends. But you can control what she hears in your home. Her tone will mimic your own. Once again, it's up to us to provide her with the right model.

Effective Listening

I used to tell my students they needed to use their listening behavior. Where should your eyes be? Where should your hands be? What should your mouth be doing? Effective listening is respectful listening, but it doesn't end there. Effective listening is also active listening. While you listen are you just waiting for your turn to talk again? Active listening asks questions, makes comments, and acknowledges understanding. How are you at effective listening? Your child is learning this skill from you.

In our lives, we will spend more time listening than almost any other activity—more than reading, writing, or even speaking (believe it or not). Listening is a skill we can teach. But learning to be still long enough to listen is an important prerequisite. When our children were very young (18 to 24 months old), we had what we called *sit time*. Once a day I would sit them either on the floor or on the couch with a book on tape and headphones. After they got past the fact that they didn't like the headphones, I encouraged them to listen to the book on tape for five minutes. Soon, it was 10, then 15, and so on. Our goal was to teach them to sit and listen to two books on tape for approximately 30 minutes by the time they were two years old.

This activity required focus, patience, and the ability to sit still—things all children need to learn. Other early listening skills we wanted to encourage were making eye contact when speaking, standing still (not flitting from side to side when speaking), replying "Yes, Mommy," and coming immediately when called. We even began using a family whistle to gather us together when outside or in a public place. Find out what works for your family; there are many ways to develop listening behavior in young children.

When children get older, you can teach them more sophisticated listening behavior. It's important to learn how to listen with concentration even among distractions. They need to maintain eye contact with the speaker. They need to listen when someone disagrees with an opinion. They need to learn how to restate what the other person has said to ensure the speaker knows he was understood. These are all characteristics of mature listening behavior.

Classrooms can be highly distracting places. Our children must learn to listen even if someone nearby is being disruptive. Later they need to learn to listen in an auditorium setting such as what they will experience in a general education class in college. They need to learn to listen to everyone—friends, spouses, other children, and their parents. They need to be able to listen closely in their future job-training orientation. Effective listening is undoubtedly one of the strongest, most relevant assets to success in life.

Understand Your Audience

If your child is going to prepare a speech for his class, does it matter how appropriate his language is? Is his "listener" young or old, tired or happy, annoyed or ignorant? It's important to be aware and understand to whom we are speaking before we speak. Similarly, we may be talking to a friend

and go on and on about something, forgetting that our audience may not have any concern for the matter at all. We need to help children think *outside themselves* before they speak or write.

Human beings are incredibly self-centered. Maybe you've noticed! We want things *our* way, as often (and as soon) as possible. Knowing the characteristics and needs of your audience is a matter of respect. Anything else is self-serving. We shouldn't speak just to hear ourselves talk. Speak so that others will want to listen.

There are subtle clues to knowing whether or not you've gained the trust and interest of your audience. Yet not everyone is good at picking these up. Someone who is considered a "talker" has an especially difficult time attuning himself to the listener. He's too busy talking! My husband is definitely a talker. His teachers made this comment on his report card consistently every year! At this point in our marriage, we've realized he can use more obvious clues to remind him to do more listening. For instance, when we're talking with another couple at a restaurant, I might remind him he's getting long-winded by placing my hand on his knee. One-sided conversations aren't any fun for the listener. But being sensitized to the needs of your listeners is a social skill that often comes with practice.

As children have the opportunity to present an oral report or project at school, they will hopefully learn quickly what holds the interest of an audience, and what doesn't. For example, a group of 30 sixth graders right before lunch are hungry and probably antsy. (Ask a teacher—she knows!) They are more interested in watching the clock than in listening to an oral report. It will be even more difficult to gain their attention if your topic isn't relevant or is not made more relevant by the presentation. They will probably not be engaged and likely not even close to being active listeners. Below are some suggestions for making the most of such situations:

- Make eye contact with everyone in your audience.
- Be brief and to the point.

- Be enthusiastic and dynamic (but not over-the-top).
- Use visual aids.
- Ask questions to gain audience participation.
- Speak clearly and strongly.
- Speak with authority.
- Relate the subject to the audience's life.

The more practice students have speaking in public, the more finely tuned their speaking skills will become. It's not an easy skill to master for anyone. In fact it can be downright terrifying, but it sure comes in handy later in life.

Written Communication

Some people believe that the art and skill of writing has become less important in the age of computers. I disagree. What you write represents who you are—even what you write online. What do you think when you get e-mail that is full of spelling errors and inconsistencies? The mechanics of writing are just as important to conveying your message as the way you choose to write it.

Logical composition is also a matter of respecting the reader. Your message can be misunderstood or even lost if your writing isn't logical. Some people have a natural talent for writing what they mean, and others must depend on others to teach them. But even naturally talented writers must learn the mechanics. It is an art *and* a craft.

Our schools concentrate on the craft of writing. Students are tested on it. Written communication is vital to virtually every aspect of professional and social life. My husband is a sales rep for an office furniture company. Sometimes a client's first impression of him or his company comes as a result of an introductory letter. Often he asks me to check his letters to make sure they are professional, to the point, respectful of the client, and

clear. He trusts my judgment more than his own. He feels more comfortable talking than writing, so he seeks help with his letters because he knows it's important to give the right impression.

Even though our children are learning the mechanics of writing in school, there are some useful work habits to help make writing more powerful and interesting to the reader.

Read rough drafts aloud.

This first step in the editing process allows children to *hear* the mistakes their eyes might miss. Reading the draft aloud again when it is done can improve any form of writing, whether it's an essay, a research paper, or a 500-page book.

Be brief.

Strunk and White's famously brief handbook, *The Elements of Style,* advises writers to "omit needless words."[1] Even when writing long reports, you can help your child use only the words needed. The point is to get to the point. Expressing ideas in as few words as possible ensures that the message doesn't get lost.

Use simple language.

This is not to say we can't use big words, but we shouldn't use words that are excessive. Sometimes children need to be reminded that they are not writing to impress the teacher with their vocabulary. We write to communicate a message—that is all.

Use a variety of sentence types.

Most students only use one sentence type in their writing—the simple sentence—one subject and one verb. *The dog bit the boy.* Mixing in other types of sentences adds interest. Compound, complex, and compound-complex

sentences can keep the reader from falling asleep—and again, keep the message from getting lost.

Use anecdotes where appropriate.

Everyone loves a story. Even a paper about mitochondria should include at least one story. Engage the reader by starting with a paragraph about a 10-year-old boy whose little sister has been diagnosed with a mitochondrial disease. The message feels more personal and therefore more relevant. A personal message holds attention much better.

The Art and Skill of Debate

Debate intimidates many of us, yet its value supersedes the anxiety. Being able to effectively offer an opinion along with supporting evidence is a commanding skill. Debate is the ability to persuade one person to your way of thinking. Whether we know it or not, we use persuasion every day—at home, at school, and at work.

In his book *The Art of Thinking,* Vincent Ruggiero says, "Persuasive writing and speaking ask an audience to replace ideas they know and accept with ideas they have never heard before or, worse, have considered and rejected."[2] Ruggiero offers five guidelines for persuasive communication:

Use evidence effectively.

Evidence is the relevant facts, your experiences, and any observations you find helpful. Children (and many parents) need to realize that they can't answer an objection intelligently simply with the words, "Because I said so." Facts, experiences, and observations are what your audience needs to know to be persuaded to your way of thinking. Of course, it is best to start giving and expecting evidence from your children as early as possible. When our son Charles wants to do something differently from the way I asked, I ask for his reason. His automatic answer is usually, "I don't know," or, "I just want to—that's all." Yet there are reasons for everything we do or say. Help your child to identify these and expect evidence for his opinions. This may be a new habit for you, but it's worth the effort. Now I may say to Charles, "If you want to convince me of _____, you need to give me at least one good reason why." Take the time to stand there and expect an answer with evidence. Eventually children develop this habit and automatically offer reasons for their thinking. It's a habit they can use throughout their lives.

Respect your audience.

When we disagree over ideas, there is a good chance someone may get angry. And once a person gets angry, they can no longer hear what you have to say because they have already decided it's irrelevant. In *The Art of Thinking*, Ruggerio writes, "We can easily conclude that those who disagree with us are stupid or villainous or both. That kind of attitude not only poisons debate but also makes persuasion difficult or impossible."[3] This often happens between husbands and wives, but teenagers are also quick to become angry when there is disagreement. Here, it's important to distinguish between the idea and the person. Remember that the person with whom you are arguing is someone who deserves your respect. If you try to mask your disrespect, there's a good chance they will see through it. Don't let controversial issues take over. State your opinion and realize that with this issue, people are bound to have disagreements. The important thing is to respect the people with whom you are communicating.

Begin with the familiar.

Debate or persuasion requires a common starting point. Your audience needs a point on which to base their agreement, preferably a point of familiarity. Common ground is a positive first impression that builds both trust and credibility between you and your audience. Sometimes, the only familiar starting point is to agree that this is a difficult issue.

Select the most appropriate tone.

We discussed this issue earlier. It's always good to be calm, objective, and courteous in choosing when you speak.

Answer all significant objections.

When you've chosen an issue of some relevance, there will likely be objections to what you have to say. Some are valid and some are not, but both need to be addressed or they will be obstacles to your case. Try to address all objections directly and within the flow of your presentation. However, if you spend too much time on objections, they can dominate and distract from your other, more effective persuasive elements.

Socratic Questioning

This age-old method of exploring comprehension gives us the opportunity to ask *why*. Some of us were discouraged from asking this question when we were little. Maybe it caused unsuspecting parents to have to dig deeper and think harder. Children tend to do this naturally, and it should be encouraged as much as possible. It draws out new foundations for our conclusions and helps us evaluate the opinions of others. Based on Socrates' teaching, this method of questioning can allow for a quick evaluation of what a person does or doesn't know. And characteristically, Socratic questions are almost always open-ended, that is, they don't require one correct answer.

Learning how to ask and answer these kinds of questions fosters critical thinking, evaluation, and knowledge application in your child. It challenges assumptions, clarifies issues, and identifies students' strengths and weaknesses. There are a variety of resources available to encourage Socratic dialogue and questioning, but most effective is simply working to implement the process in your daily interactions. You probably already use some of these questions in everyday life, but try these when probing for a child's motives:

- *Clarification of Assumptions* You seem to be assuming that _____; what could we assume instead? Do I understand you correctly? How do you justify that position.
- *Clarification of Reasoning* How does that relate to the issue? Could you put it another way? Could you give an example? Could you explain that further? Can you explain your reasons? What do you mean by _____? Why do you say that? Why do you think that is? What led you to that belief? How could we find out if you are right?
- *Viewpoint and Perspective* What would someone who disagrees say? What is an alternative viewpoint? How are your idea and mine alike?
- *Implications and Consequences* What are you implying with that? But if that happened, what would happen as a result?[4]

With a little more intentional use, Socratic questioning can be yet another tool for you to encourage effective communication in your child.

We all begin with questions. As we grow up, we tend to redirect those questions that make us uncomfortable. We *learn* to dislike uncertainty. Exploration and risk-taking are both natural elements your child already possesses for success. As you help your child to ask these questions about everything she does, hears, and sees, you may find yourself rediscovering your natural capacity to wonder as well. Life, terrible events, and issues can desensitize us all, and we stop asking why. But finding out why is a good thing, a lesson that parents should not forget.

Finally, we all know it takes practice, practice, and practice to become an effective communicator. The more opportunity we have to spend time in conversation with our children, the better we will help them form meaningful, persuasive, and constructive communication skills for their future.

Your Turn to Learn

Are you an effective communicator? Take the time now to evaluate your status. Target areas of improvement for yourself and practice good communication habits with your spouse, friends, and family.

- Are you often misunderstood?
- Are you an active listener?
- Are you aware of your own tone of voice when talking to your children or spouse?
- Are there times when you talk too much and aren't aware of the needs of your listeners?
- Do you avoid confrontations because you don't feel confident that you can argue effectively?
- Do you welcome or discourage *why* questions from your children?

Connections

Learning how to communicate effectively can improve your relationships—both personal and professional. Since none of us are mind readers, we depend on the spoken and written word to get our message across. There is a time to talk, and a time to listen. Learning to listen makes us better learners.

✔ Home

Do your children come when they are called the first time? If they heard you and ignored you or didn't answer, they should be trained to reply, "I'm coming!" When you give instructions, they should look at you and respond, "Yes, Mom," or "Yes, Dad." Then you know they're listening, and you can hold them accountable for what you've said.

Show & Tell: We are all easily distracted. Cell phones and e-mail may seem to have improved our communication, but they also distract us from listening to our children. When you're having a conversation with your child, intercept the distractions as much as possible. Turn off the television or cell phone. When you do, they will talk more—and they won't have the opportunity to say that *you* don't listen.

✔ School

Parent/teacher communication is just as important as student/teacher communication. Does your child feel comfortable going to his teacher for help? If not, it may be because he doesn't know how. Encourage him to ask questions. Let the teacher know about his difficulty, so that she can encourage him more.

> *Show & Tell:* How are your parent/teacher communication skills? Make sure you always get information from the teacher and not from other parents or students. Be courteous. Speak respectfully to and about the teacher. Our children are listening.

✔ Work

Listening to what the boss expects of you and speaking up for yourself are important communication skills on the job. In preparing your child for her first job, encourage her to ask questions. For example, she may not realize that she can question a manager's decision, but she should be able to explain to her employer if the schedule doesn't work for her or your family.

> *Show & Tell:* Do you speak up to your employer when necessary? What if he doesn't pay you on time? What if he expects you to work on your day off? Let your children know how you would handle these situations in an effective way if they arose.

Family Activity

Try these two activities to encourage effective communication.

Copycat Drawing

This activity helps everyone learn to give clear, concise directions to achieve a common goal. One person draws a simple picture and then directs others in drawing the same picture—without showing them what he's drawn. Each person follows the artist's directions and when finished, they compare drawings. Discover where the artist was effective and ineffective in communicating the directions. Sometimes the drawings will look nothing like the original. Once everyone has had a chance to be the artist, discuss ways in which everyone can work on explaining the directions better.

Stories with Holes

This activity comes from a book series written by Nathan Levy, which is great for learning how to ask effective questions.[5]

The object is to lead your children to discovering the answer using as few questions as possible. Introduce the story, saying something like this: "I am going to tell you a story with a hole in it—that is, an important part of the story is missing. Listen carefully so you can find the hole. After I read the story you may ask only yes or no questions."

Story #1: *The man was afraid to go home, because the man with the mask was there.*

Answer: The man with the mask was a catcher in a baseball game; the other man a base runner. The word *home* refers to home plate.

Story #2: *John and Mary are on the floor. There are pieces of broken glass and a puddle of liquid on the floor as well. Mary is dead.*

Answer: John, the cat, knocked over the fishbowl of Mary, the fish.

Chapter Nine

A Confident Leader

"Speak up and judge fairly; defend the rights of the poor and needy."
—PROVERBS 31:9

"Follow the leader!" my cousin commanded during a forbidden walk in the woods. I always followed Roxanne wherever she went because she was so cool! But I was a little worried that we'd get caught playing in the woods behind my grandmother's house. We were warned once, and I wasn't a rule breaker, but Roxanne made it fun to follow her.

My younger sister and I did the best we could to keep up with our cousin. We followed her over boulders, under low-lying branches, and on top of fallen trees. We jumped over a small chasm and climbed down a relatively high rock wall into the pit below. It was deeper than I estimated and filled with fine gray sand. Soon, exhausted and disinterested in our game of follow-the-leader, we decided to head back to the house.

But now we had to climb out of the pit. The walls weren't as easy to climb up as they had been to scurry down. Every time we gained a foothold, it filled in with sand and we slid back to the bottom. Roxanne had somehow found a way out. She stood atop the pit and laughed at my sister and me covered with sand and out of breath. Then she was gone!

My sister, Amy, started to cry. We tried to find suitable spots to climb out and realized through many efforts that she was too small to climb out by herself, and I wasn't nearly coordinated enough to maintain both our footing. Eventually we sat, afraid Roxanne wouldn't come back for us before dark.

I realized we were doomed no matter what Roxanne did. If she'd gone for help, we were in trouble for being in the woods. If she didn't, we were alone, in the dark with little hope of being found.

Why had I followed her? Why hadn't I just said we'd stay in the yard and play? Not only had I followed the wrong person, but my sister had followed me as well! Roxanne did eventually bring back help, so we made it out, but it was the last time I ever followed her anywhere!

Are children born effective leaders, or is it a skill that can be learned? Anyone with more than one child knows that some are natural leaders and some are decidedly followers. With "follower children" we worry that they will choose to follow the wrong leaders. Will they be easily swayed by peer pressure? Will they make choices in life they will later regret? With our "leader children," we worry, are they aware of the responsibility of leadership? Are they leaders who are worth following? Have they acquired the leadership skills they'll need to be successful?

Leaders have influence that affects their achievement of goals. Effective leaders must collaborate and cooperate with others to enable solutions rather than simply supply their own solution. According to John Maxwell in his book *The 21 Indispensable Qualities of a Leader*, "Leaders are effective because of who they are on the inside—in the qualities that make them up as people. And to go to the highest level of leadership, people have to develop these traits from the inside out."[1]

Effective Leaders Know the Impact of Behaviors

We are all followers, and we are all leaders. Parents lead children; children lead other children. Whose attitudes, styles, and behaviors do you follow? Your parents? A person in your community? A spiritual leader or pastor? I think whom we decide to follow changes throughout our lives. Sometimes we follow the wrong person. Who are our heroes? Who are our children's heroes? These are people whom we emulate.

I became a teacher because of my own first-grade teacher—I wanted to be just like her! And when I became a teacher, I had the pleasure of hearing from former students who said I had a great influence on their lives. What a privilege that is.

It's important for parents to know whom they follow so that they are aware of the kind of leaders they'll become. Have you ever discovered that you no longer wanted to be associated with a particular leader, and then actively pursued a new one? It is our beliefs, our points of view in this world that lead us.

Our hearts will follow our minds. Once your mind convinces your heart something is true, your decisions and your actions will lead your children. This is where leadership training is most effective. What kind of leader are you? How can parents provide the best possible model for children?

Effective Leaders Assert Personal Values

This is where effective communication comes in. People follow when they know what you want and where you're going, and your message is clear, simple, and precise. Leaders know their audience and believe in what they say.

It's show-and-tell time again. Your personal values, ideas, and points of view are on display. If we tell our children not to smoke, yet we have trouble not lighting up, what message does it send? Credibility is crucial to effective leadership. Even potentially life-changing messages get lost if the leader is not credible. I feel the burden of this ideal when I tell my children no sweets before dinner, and proceed to sneak a couple of Oreos for myself. Chip feels it when he makes the boys limit their television time, but then they find him sitting in front of "The Speed Channel."

It may be true that parents have the right to do what they want, but we need to remember that with freedom comes responsibility. If you make enough of these "good-for-me-but-not-for-you" choices, eventually your credibility with your children will be compromised. It's an incredibly humbling truth!

Effective Leaders Listen

Leaders don't lead alone. They lead either a nation or one person as a member of a group, successfully interacting with and employing the skills of others. Leaders do this in a variety of ways, the most important of which is *listening*.

Listening is the equal partner to speaking in effective communication. A leader who listens never lacks for followers. John Maxwell says that we have two purposes in listening: To connect with people, and to learn.[2] Connecting with others requires that we take the time to get to know them on a deep level. One can even hear what a person says without knowing from where his opinions come. To know why they think the way they do, we have to find out. If we dismiss their opinions, in our quest to get things done, we may run right over the very person who can accomplish our visions.

In a family, there is the same dynamic, often as diverse as any workplace. You must take the time to get to know why your children say and do the things they do. You trained them to behave, but they struggle with peer issues. They might develop strong spiritual beliefs you don't share. Whatever the reasons, learn to listen more. Change your schedule if you have to. Find the time. If you're too busy to listen, you're too busy.

Interpersonal skill is another tool for good listening. Good "people skills" is the more common term. According to Maxwell, being adept in social situations means understanding, loving, and helping.

"The ability to look at each person, understand him, and connect with him is a major factor in relational success," writes Maxwell.[3] People don't react in the same ways to a given situation, they don't value the same things, and they don't believe the same things. An effective leader will become sensitive to these differences.

It may be that your child needs to change his leadership style. A good indication is how he or she responds to your leading.

Growing up, I was a sensitive child. My sister was generally prideful and argumentative. Because of this, my mother did not discipline us the same. She tells the story of how when I was three, she made me sit on the couch for a time-out, and I was devastated. My sister, on the other hand, required a heavier punishment. My mother knew that my sister and I were not the same so she didn't treat us the same. I found that was useful when I had two boys of my own who are just as different as my sister and I were.

An effective leader loves others. No one on this earth is here to live in isolation. We're wired to be in relationship with one another. If we don't love one another, it's impossible to serve them. How are your relationships? Is there someone in your life right now who is hurting because of you? Strive to restore that relationship. How can you add value to the lives of your friends and family? Think of ways to show compassion, love, and care for those who have been placed in your life.

Love is focusing on what you can give—not what you can get.

Are you a taker or a giver? Are you aware of the interests and needs of those who follow you? Think of ways to help your child achieve his own goals. Let him see you reaching out to help others. Go ahead and help even when you don't feel like it, and your child will learn a valuable lesson about true leadership.

Effective Leaders Know Their Leadership Style

Books have been written about the different leadership styles, but surely each style has qualities that are as individual as people themselves. There are tests you can take to determine which one you gravitate toward. But one style is generally regarded as the most effective: the style of *servant leadership*. Eugene B. Habecker says, "The true leader serves. Serves people. Serves their best interests, and in so doing will not always be popular, may not always impress. But because true leaders are motivated by loving concern rather than a desire for personal glory, they are willing to pay the price."[4]

Putting the needs of others first may not be easy, yet it is essential to leading them well. Firefighters put the needs of others first. Aren't we glad? Teachers put the needs of others first. Great leaders lead us by providing examples of how we should live as well. Even still, servant leadership is difficult to find today. We all know some bad examples. But anticipating the needs of others originates with an attitude as much as bad service extends from a bad attitude.

To give everything for others' benefit: This is what makes leaders truly effective. So encourage children to truly listen to people, to care for them, to stop seeking their own way, and start serving others. Those who would be great must be humble and be a servant to everyone.

Effective Leaders Have a Distinct and Well-Defined Vision

Leaders need to have a vision for the future. We think of a "visionary" as a gifted leader with inspired insight. But *Webster's Dictionary* defines a *visionary* as "one whose ideas or projects are impractical: [a] dreamer." What a visionary sees as a goal for the future may seem impractical, but it is an essential element in developing great leaders. Children are natural visionaries. They don't see the obstacles to their dreams. They don't censor their ideas as being unrealistic. To help children gain insight about the future, parents must often first reform their own thinking.

Since you lead your children, having a vision for your family and your own life is a necessity in effectively modeling visionary leadership. If you've never developed a vision for your family, begin by asking yourself the following four questions:

1. What gifts do I have that can positively influence my family? Do you have a unique gift or calling of some sort? Are you an "encourager"? How do you show love; do you know your "love language"?[5] If you are gifted in service, then maybe your family vision includes serving others outside the home. If you have the gift of giving, then maybe your family vision includes charitable contributions to your community. Learn to recognize the gifts in your family members. A family vision reveals itself when you see what gifts, talents, and abilities you have to work with.

2. What about my childhood shapes my parenting style? Key events in your past drive you forward in the present. Do you want to duplicate the kind of home in which you were brought up? Or do you want to create a completely opposite environment for your family? Regrets and memories both inform and inspire our visions for the future.

3. How can I show that I value my family members? Your vision should go beyond just what you can accomplish—serving others shows that you value the people around you. Look for little ways to show appreciation of, care for, and interest in the members of your family.

4. Does my family vision bring us together or pull us apart? If your vision is self-serving, it will drive people away. But a vision that attracts and unites people puts others' needs first. Consider how you plan a family vacation.

Do you plan with only your interests in mind and end up taking everyone along kicking and screaming? Not all family decisions must be democratic, but a selfless vision will serve others, excite them, and best utilize the gifts of everyone in the group.

One final word on encouraging children to develop vision: Allow them (and yourself) to dream. When you do, you are encouraging their future. Imagining oneself as a leader can create that reality and make people want to follow. And if a child is convinced he is a leader, he can take on anything in this world with confidence.

Isn't that what we all want for our children?

Both "leader children" and "follower children" can benefit from leadership training. All children will have the opportunity to lead, whether as a pupil, a parent, or a president. When you hug your child, remember you're shaping a future leader and his perception of what leadership is. Provide the world with a leader worth following.

Your Turn to Learn

Every day we play follow-the-leader, whether we realize it or not. The trick is to know whom you're following. Your child will follow you, so it's especially important that you know whom you're following to know where you're leading. Effective leadership is not simply based on holding the title of Mommy or Daddy.

- Are you willing to put the needs of others first, or is every day run your way?
- Do you effectively communicate your personal values and points of view?
- Are you a credible leader? Do you walk what you talk?
- Are you a good listener?
- Are you willing to serve those you lead?
- Do you have a vision for your family?

Connections

We are both leaders and followers. Our children will lead in the way we teach them, so we must be sure to give them the right examples.

✔ Home

Our children have many opportunities to demonstrate leadership: in the backyard, on the playground, on the ball field, or at a friend's house. Do they understand the responsibilities of being a good leader? Does he always take a "Me first" attitude, or does he willingly serve others and their needs?

Show & Tell: Leadership is learned in the family. Children will learn how to treat their own future spouses by watching how their parents treat one another. They will learn how to lead their own

future children by watching how we lead them. Be mindful of this awesome leadership responsibility.

✔ School

When they are in kindergarten, we can encourage our kids to be good leaders rather than followers of what "everybody else" is doing. If someone in their class chooses to disobey the teacher, children must know that they should obey the teacher, no matter what. If a child is outgoing, it is even more important that he be respectful, do his work, and treat others kindly.

> *Show & Tell*: A child's success in school is directly linked to his parent's involvement. Are you active in your child's school? This doesn't mean that you need to become president of the PTA, but you must lead your children to honor and respect their teachers by first showing them that you do as well.

✔ Work

Not every job will be a managerial position. Our children will likely spend more time as employees than employers. But even as an employee, one can demonstrate leadership skills. Other employees will watch to see how your child handles a problem or confrontation. Teach them to be mindful of what their attitudes and behaviors demonstrate to others.

> *Show & Tell*: What do you do when you witness unethical business practices in your job? Even if it draws negative attention, do you stand up for what you believe and do the right thing? Tell your children how you would handle such a situation.

Family Activity

In your house, Mom may usually plan and prepare the family meal. But every member of the family should get to do so at some time. When planning a meal, a good leader considers the needs of others before his. This requires time and patience as the meal is chosen, recipes are found, a grocery list is compiled, the meal is prepared, the table is set, and finally, the family is served.

Once a month one of our boys will plan, cook, and serve the family dinner. We started this practice when each of them turned nine. Now at 12 and 10 years old, they have each prepared dinner for their dad and me many times.

Here are some questions for children to consider in planning, preparing, and serving a family meal:

- What kind of cooking does the meal require? Can you ask for help when using the stove, oven, microwave, or grill?
- What are the favorite foods of each of your family members?
- Which day would be best for the family to eat together?
- How can you make this meal special for your family? What creative ideas do you have?
- How will the meal be served? Will you need help?
- How will the meal be presented? Even if the menu calls for hot dogs and baked beans, presentation is still important.

Younger children may need some help preparing a grocery list in advance. Help with what he needs this time, and next time see if he is able to do it himself. And always remember to compliment your child on his accomplishment and effort.

Chapter Ten

An Efficient Time Manager

"There is a time for everything, a season for every activity under heaven."
—ECCLESIASTES 3:1

As far as I can remember, my parents never set out to intentionally teach me how to manage my time. I do remember having school projects to complete, and feeling conscientious about my work. But there were also times when I failed in my responsibilities as a student and waited until the last minute to finish an assignment. Fortunately, I did not receive encouragement in my lackadaisical approach, and when I received a poor grade, I knew inside that it was what I deserved.

Yet somehow my parents instilled in me the value of time management. I can recall certain routines in our family. We did our homework at the same time every day, and we didn't go out to play, talk on the phone, or have friends over until it was finished. Television time and extracurricular activities were considered carefully against our other responsibilities. We ate together as a family every night, and Sundays were strictly for *family only*. Even when we became teenagers and were more involved with sports or clubs, it was always understood that school was to come first. In high school when I begged to be allowed to get a part-time job, I was denied. "You'll be working for the rest of your life," my parents reasoned. "There's no need to start now."

In this life, the great equalizer is time. We all are given the same 24 hours in a day, and we choose moment by moment how we will use those hours, minutes, and seconds. I've yet to meet anyone who felt they had too much time. Parents are especially aware of how quickly time passes, almost painfully so. Children sprout up like Jack's beanstalk, growing up and away from us in the blink of an eye. They will learn how to spend their time, in school and later in life, by how carefully we consider the use of our time now.

Whether or not my parents' philosophy would work in your family, every parent must make wise choices about their time. If we don't plan how we are going to spend our time, we will end up running around from one activity to another without any purpose in life. It's the difference between being a reactive person and a proactive person. A reactive person can only *react* to situations, and consequently, their lives are full of stress. On the other hand, a proactive person plans his time and is able to keep his stress level to a low roar. According to *Webster's Dictionary,* a *manager* is "one who is at the head of an undertaking." When you manage your time, it doesn't manage you.

Prioritizing is something we do throughout our lives. In fact, it happens every day, whether we realize it or not. But staying ahead of the game requires forethought and planning. And the more often you take time to evaluate your priorities, the more effective you will be as a time manager. Where you spend your time shows what you value in life. In families, it is crucial that these values are shared priorities. Ideally, the husband and wife are working toward a common vision for their family, and their daily choices line up with that vision.

Some choices are more consequential than others. When my husband, Chip, and I first married, I was working as a schoolteacher. When I became pregnant with our first child, I realized that we had never talked about what would happen after the child was born. Would I go back to work? If so, when? Would I stay home? If so, how would we afford it? This was a huge decision, one with far-reaching consequences. We talked together about what our values were and what the priority was for our new family. I was thrilled to discover that we were in agreement on this matter. We had the same priorities! We agreed that I would stay at home, but that choice had a ripple effect on many other of our daily decisions, including how to budget our money.

Your Family's Values

Every family must decide its own values. The key is communication among family members to come up with ones on which everyone can agree. Some examples might include valuing time spent together, the influence of faith, service, sharing, education, nature, friendships, finances, honesty, kindness, responsibility, or self-control.

Whether we are aware of it or not, parents communicate the family values to their children. Kids determine what is most important by how Mom and Dad spend their time and where they spend their money. (For example, my children know that I value Starbucks® coffee!)

What are your priorities for your children and family? If you've never taken the time to write it out before, now would be a great time to do so! There are three crucial elements to this process: learning how to set priorities, consider new endeavors, and say no when appropriate.

Although you may not have realized it, you have probably already used the technique of setting priorities, when you've constructed a budget or a diet plan. When setting priorities for your family, the following steps can be taken:

Step 1—*Create a list* of everything you do during the day/week/month. Write it down—all of it—even the laundry. Then ask a close friend or someone who understands what your life is like to check if you've forgotten something. You will probably be amazed at how much you actually do.

Step 2—*Compare* item by item what you're doing with your established family values. For example, if your family "values" dinner together, but each of your children goes to different activities at 5:30, three nights per week, it doesn't show that you actually value that priority. If you did, the activities at 5:30 would have been vetoed in favor of something else that didn't conflict with the family's dinnertime.

Step 3—*Cut out* the things that don't measure up to your value system. This can be a painful process. But if what you are doing doesn't fulfill your established (or newly established) family values, it should be reevaluated, and certain activities might have to go.

Step 4—*Communicate* the reasoning behind these changes with your children. They need to understand and embrace your family values. It may be difficult to train them to set their own priorities if they don't see the importance of your family's priorities. When they are trying to decide which sports or clubs to join, they'll have the ability to decide which values each serves.

Step 5—*Commit* to protecting your time. Sometimes you'll have to say no to a favor a friend asks of you; other times, your family's values would be served in doing that favor as a family. Committing to our own family's time means we don't have to do all the things others may want us to do, even if they're good things. But considering what effect the activities have will help you decide if they fit with your values. There's nothing wrong with soccer, football, music lessons, youth group, or a part-time job. But before adding any more activities to the schedule, family members must consider their motivations and the impact that activity will have on the family unit.

Time Flies!

Most of us forget how precious little time we really have with our children. You can make the most of it by modeling time management for your child. Do you wait until the last minute to get things done? Or do you plan ahead, determining how long something will take? Encourage your child to plan ahead with his or her time as well.

What kinds of skills do our children need in order to be successful at managing their time? The time required for the demands of school is their greatest challenge at this point. Most teachers try to teach students time management, either directly or indirectly with progressive assignments. But a teacher's time is limited too.

Here are five suggestions to help children manage their time successfully.

Make a schedule.

If your family is too busy, like most are, ask yourself, is there a method to the madness, or are you typically running from activity to activity, just reacting to the schedule set for you by others? School is currently your child's "job." Completion of quality work at this job should take precedence over everything else. Is there sufficient time set aside in the schedule for that to happen? Most kids today are overextended. But it's all a matter of choice: We all choose how we spend the 24 hours we are given each day. And parents should be the ones who say yes or no to the activities in which our children wish to participate. If your family is too busy, then it is up to you as the "grown-up" to change that.

One of the best ways to help students maintain a study schedule is to write down daily assignments in a planner or notebook. Many schools have their own assignment planners in an attempt to help students do this.

Set reasonable goals.

How long does a book report take in order to do it well? How many steps are involved in creating a science-fair project? Encourage children to make a plan to complete projects on time and ward off procrastination. This skill does not come naturally. In fact, they will probably even fight you on it. Yet when our children are panicking at 10:00 P.M. on a Sunday night as they realize a semester project is due the next morning, the value of a long-term plan becomes quite clear. Be involved early in the process by helping them plan their time, rather than preaching at them later, or even giving in and doing their project for them.

Arrive on time.

When children who are driven to school are late, guess what? The parents are to blame! Our children may dillydally in the morning and frustrate our already tight schedule, but if that's happening, it's up to us to get up even earlier so that their delay tactics don't make them late. If your child is the one completely responsible for getting himself to school on time, then he will need to accept whatever consequences come. But since most children are somewhat dependent upon their parents to transport them to school, this is a good time to model responsible behavior and adhere to a schedule. Teachers don't care *why* students are late, and children, not parents, are the ones punished for tardiness. Getting to school on time prepares students for the world of work where arriving late is likely to cost them their job.

Set and meet deadlines.

We all live by deadlines in one form or another. Some are self-imposed, and some are imposed by others. This summer while my children were away for two weeks at their grandparents' house, I painted all of our kitchen cabinets. My goal was to complete this project before the boys came home—it was a self-imposed deadline. Every year our children's schools hold a fundraiser in which the kids sell magazine subscriptions. If they choose to participate, they are expected to meet the school-imposed deadline. There are deadlines to apply to programs and activities. There are deadlines for subscriptions and memberships. There are a myriad of deadlines included in the college experience. There are deadlines to pay your bills. There are deadlines inherent in every occupation. Some of us responsibly meet deadlines, but some of us don't. There are rewards for those who do, and consequences for those who don't.

In order for our children to embrace the value of being an efficient time manager, we must provide them with opportunities to experience success and failure with deadlines. Beginning when they are young, we must teach our children the importance of adhering to deadlines. Early lessons take the form of learning obedience. Does your child come right away when she is called? Does he do the job you've asked him to do right away or within a specified time frame? Do you hold him accountable for obedience? Home is the initial training ground, and school is where this skill is practiced with supervision. By the time children reach college or the world of work, they begin to work with deadlines on their own.

Look for ways to increase opportunities for practice in this area. Use a timer for homework or chores. Set up a system of rewards and consequences if your child doesn't take to deadlines willingly. Work with your child's teacher to help him meet school-imposed deadlines. Is there a project coming up that you should monitor and help your child to finish on time?

Look around and point out to your child when you notice others meet or miss their deadlines. Comment on the rewards or consequences of such behavior. The next time your plane is late and your child is getting frustrated that you must all continue to wait, talk about why the airline's not meeting this deadline adversely affects the lives of others. When you all successfully get up early enough to leisurely get ready for church on

Sunday and you arrive fresh and stress-free, comment about how wonderful it felt to arrive ready to worship. I often wonder if deadlines are what really make the world go 'round.

Use entertainment wisely.

Our level of effectiveness can either increase or decrease depending upon how well we manage our time. There needs to be a balance between being too busy and not busy enough. Experts on child psychology continually tell us that our children are watching entirely too much television. In fact, a study called "Kids & Media: The New Millennium" found that kids spend the equivalent of a full workweek using media. For the study, *media* was defined as watching television, playing video games, listening to music, watching movies, reading books or magazines, and surfing the Internet. "The typical American child spends an average of more than 38 hours a week—nearly five and a half hours a day—consuming media outside of school." According to the study, many children have multimedia bedrooms, and the family television is on during dinner. The most poignant finding was that many parents were "not exercising much control over their children's media use." There seemed to be no rules.[1]

The attraction of media is very strong—for all of us. But our children watch how we spend our time. Of course, you should look at how you yourself use media with a critical eye before you instigate rules for your children. Do you watch too much television, or are you online too much? I know I should change some of my habits. You can curb your media appetite by eliminating the unnecessary influences.

If you value time together, then an excessive use of media will definitely hinder your fulfilling that priority. Remember: It's important to measure the cost of your activities by whether or not they add to the family's values.

Another consequence of unwise time management is the tendency

toward inactivity and poor nutrition. In America, child obesity is at an all-time high. If we don't monitor our children's time in front of a screen, they might never go outside! If we eat dinner in front of the television on a regular basis, it is likely a quick meal and therefore not as nutritious. Limiting *screen time* (including television, computer, video games, and movies) is the first step; enforcing *outside time* is the next.

It may be hard to believe you have to schedule time for your child to go play outside, but it's a sign of the times. Playing a sport or physical education at school does not count as "outside time." The point isn't just physical exercise. Outside time is unstructured time outside, being creative to come up with things to do, with or without friends. If your child owns a bicycle, expect him to ride it. If you built a tree house or a fort, he should spend time in it or modify it himself. When he says he's bored, tell him to give it time. He'll find something creative to do.

Time Management Takes Time

Most likely you are a parent of a school-age child. Right now success in school is probably a concern of yours. Success in school often leads to success in life, and we all want our children to lead successful, fulfilled adult lives. With the rising academic standards and ever-present school reforms, it takes the united front of both teachers and parents to set children up to succeed.

Tom Loveless, the director of the Brown Center on Educational Policy, says that "children in the United States don't devote much time to learning outside of the classroom."[2] Learning takes time. We all know that when we learn a new skill, it takes time and repetitive practice. Loveless says, "Good policies will help, but schools cannot do it alone. No amount of money or legislation can change the central tenet of learning: The family is the single most important influence."[3]

Success takes time. Helping children learn how to manage their time is our job. There are five distinct areas in which parents can exert influence in how children spend their time:

Homework

It *is* necessary and essential for success. According to studies, children generally do not have too much.

Socializing with friends

Your influence as parents must outweigh the influence of friends. If we want our children to embrace our values, we must spend more time with them than they do with their friends. Of course, there is need for balance in this area.

Extracurricular activities

If your child's activities interfere with his schoolwork, it's time to cut back. Extracurricular activities are necessary for certain areas of development, but for struggling students, they may be too much. It's a tough decision to make, but too much time away from a child's studies can rob him of a successful future.

Television

As I mentioned before, the key is monitoring and limiting, not necessarily strictly forbidding television.

Part-time jobs

Teens are especially susceptible to working too many hours at a part-time job. Especially during the school year, the number of hours they work should be cut down. Unfortunately, teens can easily find themselves unable to control the amount of hours their employer assigns, so it's important to

help them find a job that values their schooling enough to work within their schedule.

As parents, we are our families' ultimate time managers. Most likely, we are all making progress in this area. But there may be some situations we are struggling to hold together. We must take control, be the "grown-up," and learn to say no.

No to activities that rob time from your family.

No to responsibilities that do not carry out your family's values.

No to excessive media influence.

No to other distracting influences that do not share your family's values.

Time is too precious to waste. In so many ways, it is all we have.

✏— Your Turn to Learn

We have all been given the gift of time, and all of us are accountable for how we spend it. The word *manager* comes from the Latin word *manus*, which means "by hand," meaning, you do it yourself. Time shouldn't rule you— you should rule time! Consider some areas in which you can improve your time management skills:

- Have you set your priorities as a family?
- Do you feel in a rush much of the time?
- Are you spending more time in the car shuffling children from activity to activity than you spend at home?
- Does your spouse think his or her needs are being met?
- Do you say yes to requests before you've taken the necessary time to consider them?
- Do you frequently miss deadlines or ask for them to be extended?
- Do you have time to relax with your children?
- Are you overwhelmed by daily tasks, such as maintaining your home?
- Are you willing to make the changes necessary to restore balance in your life?

Connections

An efficient time manager makes time meaningful for himself and others. He is not nearly as stressed as someone who doesn't manage his time well. He can be counted on to meet deadlines and routinely sets them for himself.

✔ Home

Deadlines, due dates, and appointments are a big part of daily life. Children need to first learn and then respond to the time limits

imposed by others before they can learn to work independently by setting them for themselves. Encourage your child to keep the needs of others in mind when meeting a deadline. Hold him accountable with rewards and consequences.

Show & Tell: An early experience most children have with deadlines is returning a library book on time. Point out the due date of the book, mark it on your family calendar, and keep the library books in a safe place. Make sure they are returned on time. If you don't, make sure your child understands that there is a penalty for being late. As he gets older you can hold him accountable for his own late fines. Returning a rented movie or video game can be handled in a similar manner.

✔ School

In school, deadlines abound. Make it a point to become aware of your child's project or report due dates. Children won't know how to budget their time to complete the assignment unless we teach them.

Show & Tell: If you volunteer at your child's school, there's a good chance you have a task that has a deadline. Let your child see you work to meet that deadline. What would the consequences be if you were late? Would anyone be disappointed? Would teachers be able to make up what you didn't do? When your child gets an assignment, help her allocate the time to complete it. Daily homework is the perfect training ground for this expectation.

✔ Work

You've heard it said: Time is money. If someone is late, it costs him or her something. Money is earned for time spent on the job. Wages suffer for time lost off of the job.

Show & Tell: If you aren't already doing it, you might consider paying your child for unusual chores, according to his age and ability. Post the rates on the refrigerator, and help your child log time spent on a particular job to be paid at the end of the week (or two). If your child already holds a part-time job, make sure she shares the schedule with you so you can help her to be on time. Once you see her capability at setting and meeting personal deadlines, you will know you're no longer needed. The value of a punctual worker cannot be overemphasized.

Family Activity

Spending meaningful time together becomes more of a priority as your children get older. However, what parents think is "meaningful" and what kids think is "meaningful" rarely coincide.

The Boys & Girls Clubs of America presented their recommendations for making family time meaningful and memorable in a recent survey.[4]

F—Focus on children.

Getting focused is a challenge. We are too easily distracted by the demands of our day. Taking the time to really focus on your child, looking at him, and really listening when he talks are so important. Attend her sporting event and actually watch. (Don't talk on your cell phone or read a book!) Spend time with him without interruptions such as the TV or the computer.

A—Ask them.

Don't orchestrate elaborate activities. All your child usually wants is just to play with you. Ask your child what *he* would like to do. You might be surprised at how simple his suggestions are.

M—Make it fun.

Kids just wanna have fun! You may think that going to a museum is both fun and educational—and thereby a good use of time. But can you make it more fun? Even preparing dinner can be a fun event with the right creative props. Wear aprons or chef's hats and design your time around what your child enjoys.

I—Interact (don't just watch).

Kids love it when we come to watch them in a sport or performance. But they love it even more when we participate. Don't just go watch your child play baseball—play catch with him outside. Don't just watch your child act in the school play—help her with her lines or write a new play that you can perform together.

L—Listen.

Learn to stop what you're doing and just listen—really listen. What is your child saying? What are you seeing in his or her attitude or behavior? Time spent listening is never wasted.

Y—Young at heart.

Seek out fun activities you can do together. Go for a bike ride, bake cookies, create scrapbooks, tend gardens, or build models together. Having fun together keeps you young.

Chapter Eleven

A Self-Assessor

"Do not think of yourself more highly than you ought,
but rather think of yourself with sober judgment. ..."
—ROMANS 12:3

Fifth grade started out with great promise for our younger son, Charles. This would be his first full year back in school after four years of homeschooling. The first two weeks were pleasant enough. But by the end of the third week there was a problem. Hoping to get to know Charles's new teacher better, I met him at the classroom door when the kids were dismissed.

"Did Charles tell you where he sits now?" his teacher asked, raising her eyebrows and hoping I'd venture a guess.

"No," I said and then looked at my son for the answer.

"I sit right next to the teacher's desk now," he said, without missing a beat.

"He's a talker. But today he continued to talk when I was talking," his teacher explained.

As a former teacher I knew this was a cardinal sin! Students should never talk when the teacher is talking! I felt my stature shrink by at least four inches as I stood there with his teacher. I scanned my memory looking for a lesson I had somehow forgotten to teach my son. At that moment, I wondered what else would happen this year to test the life lessons we'd been so careful to teach our children. Would they stand firm or be swept away by the tide of peer pressure?

Two days later when I picked Charles up, his teacher reported that his behavior was exemplary. She was allowing him to return to his "pod," among the other children.

"I don't want to go back to my pod," Charles piped up.

"Maybe you should think about each seating arrangement and decide which one won't tempt you to talk out of turn," I smiled as I offered him a measure of control over his own destiny.

After considering each option, Charles held firm. "No. I'll work much better alone, Mrs. Sanchez."

His teacher and I were both speechless.

Later Mrs. Sanchez told me it was obvious Charles knew his strengths and weaknesses. She said it was a sign of unusual maturity. I, of course, wasn't so sure. But after a few intentionally direct conversations, I learned a little more about my son.

"Mom, I can be so easily distracted, especially by my friends. I have a lot of friends in class, so there really isn't a safe place to sit," he explained.

I silently prayed that this small sign of maturity wasn't an anomaly, but an emerging pattern for our younger child. The ability to see himself and realistically evaluate his abilities, strengths, and weaknesses was the key he most needed to grow into a productive adult. My husband's greatest desire—as well as my own—was that both of our children would know themselves and live honestly from that knowledge.

You've heard it said, maybe you've even said it yourself: Perception is everything. What you perceive to be true, to you at least, is true. Therefore, what you perceive to be true about yourself is (or will soon become) true. In my teacher preparation program, one of the things I learned and never forgot was the power of a *self-fulfilling prophecy*. In 1957, Robert Merton, a professor of sociology at Columbia, wrote that the self-fulfilling prophecy occurs when "a false definition of the situation evokes a new behavior which makes the original false conception come true."[1] In other words, once an expectation is set forth, *even if it isn't true*, we will act as though that expectation is true. The result often becomes a true behavior, through the power of positive belief. For children to know themselves, it is of utmost importance that what they believe about themselves is true before they make it so!

For better or worse, what children come to believe about themselves is largely determined by what others say about them. As parents, we are the first "others" to shape their thinking. If we say they are capable, they believe it. But if we say they are not, they will live down to that expectation. Parents are the first of such influences, but others will define a child's perception as well. Teachers, extended family members, coaches, and especially peers all play different roles in this sphere of influence.

By the time a child reaches the fifth grade, he usually has reached the "logic" stage of development and begins to question others' expectations (see chapter five). At this stage children are finally able to identify their own feelings, and parents can build on that ability by asking them to put what they are feeling into words: "Are you frustrated?" "Are you angry?" "Are you confused?" A child who can accurately identify his feelings is ready to move on to becoming a *self-assessor*.

Self-Assessors Know Their Strengths and Weaknesses

Logic dictates that the better we know ourselves, the better we will be able to use our talents to achieve our goals. Because we all learn in different ways and have different strengths and weaknesses, we need to help children discover the things within themselves that are both helping and hindering their progress.

Most traditional classrooms are run with the auditory learner in mind. Often, children who are visual or kinesthetic (tactile) learners struggle to gain meaning from the school day. Ideally, teachers should teach with a variety of strategies in order to reach all children; however, this is not always realistic. If students and parents can recognize their own learning styles, they will be better able to cope with whatever atmosphere in which they find themselves.

Understanding how you learn will help you seek out the necessary skills for your success. There has been much written on the subject of learning styles and multiple intelligence theory. An easy way to distinguish your own is to listen to the complaints when you interact with others who have different learning styles:

- Auditories often complain that kinesthetics don't *listen*.
- Visuals think auditories don't *pay attention* to them because they don't *make eye contact*.
- Kinesthetics complain that auditory and visual people are *insensitive*.

Do you ever hear these complaints in your family?

Our children need to be able to take an honest look at how they work and what changes are necessary in order to improve. This isn't always easy, but start early with little things and they will learn. For example, begin asking, "Is this your neatest handwriting?" or "Have you included every type of big cat in your report?" Whether your child is highly gifted or struggles for every good grade, he needs to be able to take a true inventory of his strengths, weaknesses, and talents.

Some of us are naturally more introspective than others. My husband claims he is basically shallow and that's why he doesn't think about how he feels about things. Yet even he is aware of his strengths and weaknesses and can communicate them—so he's not as shallow as he pretends to be! He knows that he's very organized in his habits and in his thinking, but he knows he doesn't have the gift of teaching, even when it comes to teaching our boys how to play a simple game. Chip eventually learned to recognize his strengths and weaknesses and not become defensive about them. But it takes maturity to see where you are and where you need to improve.

If you've never taken a multiple intelligence inventory, set aside a few minutes now to do so. There's one provided in the appendix at the back of this book. (You will also find a children's inventory for your child to complete.) Once you've recognized your and your child's strengths, weaknesses, and individual learning styles, you may find areas in which you could make adjustments in the way you interact and encourage your child's improvement.

Self-Assessors Engage in Self-Reflection

Helping your child to keep a journal as well as periodic conferencing with him will help him learn to reflect on how and why he's doing something. The key is to check in with your children often so that (1) your input is considered "normal" and is not intimidating to them, and (2) they learn that taking time out for reflection is a valuable process. By doing this, you are likely to notice an increase in responsible behavior and improvement over time. Our younger child, now 11, told me recently at one of our "conferences" that he realized it was better to do as much as he could during the school day because the teacher would be there if he needed help and that he would have less homework after school. For him this was a true epiphany! His in-class, on-task behavior improved dramatically after his self-reflection and discovery.

Some of us reflect better in written form, and some do better verbally. Again, your child's learning preferences will determine the method with which he is most comfortable. Don't try to force your way on him. Look at each conference as an opportunity to really listen to your child's heart and offer practical, non-judgmental advice.

Self-Assessors Identify and Eliminate Obstacles

Something will inhibit your progress every day of your life. Sometimes these obstacles are beyond your control, but others you can change, even eliminate. Unfortunately, obstacles easily frustrate children. A young child's first reaction to a formidable obstacle may be to lose his temper. Some children prefer to give up on their goals when confronted with an impediment, but others will stubbornly push forward until the obstacle breaks.

A child's personality develops at a very young age. When nine-month-old babies have obstacles that impede their progress, how they handle them can tell you whether they have a strong will or a compliant one. Remember when your child learned to stand, just before he learned to walk? When he wanted to go from standing next to the couch over to the toy on the floor four feet away, did he cry when he realized he couldn't get there from where he was? Or did he drop to the floor and begin to crawl to the toy instead?

As children grow, obstacles become more formidable. Our older son has always been a perfectionist. If he wasn't confident that he could succeed in his initial attempt, he would prefer not to try at all. There were many things he conquered easily and quickly, but other things—such as riding a bicycle—provided an imposing obstacle. When something took longer than he wanted for him to master, encouragement on our part kept him trying.

When children are young, parents can help by identifying the obstacle. But when the child is old enough to see the obstacles for themselves, it becomes natural for them to try to overcome it.

Here is a brief list of some "sample hindrance statements"—physical, mental, and character issues—which may be holding your child back.

- I am frightened by this task.
- I failed when I tried this task in the past.
- I don't have the time it takes to complete this task.

- I don't have the skill I need to complete this task.
- I don't have the support I need to complete this task.
- I don't have the money I need to complete this task.
- I am confused as to what this task requires.
- I don't want to complete this task.

Do *you* have something you feel hindered from doing? What is getting in your way? Maybe you want to exercise more. Maybe your home isn't as orderly as you'd like. Maybe your job isn't fulfilling. Maybe a friendship or a family relationship isn't going smoothly. Maybe you're not paying off your debt as quickly as you had hoped. Whatever it is, stop for a moment and consider what is impeding your progress. While there are always outside considerations, more often the things that truly hinder us are inside of ourselves. We must be willing to take a good, hard look in the mirror.

Many times, children aren't mature enough to look in the mirror honestly, without seeing a distorted view of themselves. Remember, it's all about perception, and if he believes his mirror reflects the truth, he won't know it is distorted. Whether he is too hard on himself or wouldn't take himself seriously to save his life, it's important to help your child look into a clear, distortion-free mirror. Then when he considers what hinders his progress he will have a realistic perception and from that, be able to design a logical plan of action.

Self-Assessors Develop a Plan for Improvement

Identifying hindrances and moving past them are two very different tasks. In order to move beyond obstacles, we must find ways to improve both our abilities and our circumstances. For example, your child may want to play on the soccer team but may discover he's not skilled enough. To overcome this problem, he will have to pinpoint his weaknesses and make a plan to improve. It is much the same with improving grades in school, job performance, or even one's character! Children must be trained to look for ways to improve.

Sometimes parents demand instant improvement. Our critical eye focuses on a particular weakness in our child and we point it out much too quickly. No one is guiltier of this than I am! When one of my boys doesn't complete his chores, I become frustrated and wonder, *How many times do I have to show him how to do it?* A wise friend once answered my question for me: "As many times as it takes, Vicki. That's your job." She was right. And after I picked myself off the floor from that blow of truth, I recommitted myself to my children's growth. My question then became, *How will they improve if I don't take the time to show them?*

When children face their own less-than-perfect selves, we want them to be able to make improvements. During the time they live in our homes we are there to show them how to do this, not do it for them. If you hold them accountable and guide them toward change, you will be doing them a great favor. And one day they will thank you for it!

Here are some questions to ask your child that will facilitate the self-reflection process:

- How can you get your chores done sooner so you can go out to play?
- What will help you concentrate better when you do your homework?
- How can I help you be better prepared to go to school in the morning?
- What do you need to learn to be a better baseball player?
- How can you do a better job mowing Mrs. Smith's lawn so she'll pay you the next time?
- What would make it easier for you to play with your brother?

Let your child come up with ways he can improve himself, and then support his choice. If what he proposed doesn't work, talk about possible alternatives and encourage him to keep trying. The goal is for them to face challenges prepared and able to accept and overcome them.

Your Turn to Learn

Ask yourself the following questions and see how you rate as a self-assessor.

0	1	2	3	4	5
never					frequently

1. I realistically assess my strengths and weaknesses.
2. I am aware of my personal learning style.
3. I consider how well I am doing certain tasks on a regular basis.
4. I can readily identify obstacles.
5. I desire to improve my character, my relationships with others, and my performance on certain tasks.
6. I am willing to re-evaluate my current state to see if I am progressing in the desired areas of my life.

Connections

Even though self-assessment is generally a solitary pursuit, the results of such an assessment will have an effect on those around us. Our performance at home, at school, and on the job, and consequently our relationships with the people there, can be improved by conscious, directed reflection about our abilities. And although perfection isn't possible to achieve, a willingness to accept constructive criticism and a desire to improve can go a long way toward beginning to develop this mature habit.

✔ Home

A good place to help children learn to assess themselves is with chores. Children must first be trained on how to complete the chore, and parents must then ask questions: "Did you wipe the table after clearing it?" "Did you pick your towel up off the bathroom floor?" Contrary to popular

belief, this is not nagging! It is attention to detail, a necessary element in self-assessment.

Show & Tell: As you model the concept of self-assessment for your child, pay attention to how you do your own chores. After you mowed the lawn, did you pick up the clippings? After you ate breakfast, did you put your dishes in the dishwasher? Look at what you do and find ways in which you could improve. And if you're really brave, ask your children to hold you accountable!

✔ School

At school, improvement is the name of the game. Skills are learned and constantly put to the test to push the level of proficiency. You can always tell when a child has taken responsibility for his own learning habits, because he expresses a desire to improve.

Show & Tell: Parent/teacher conferences aren't the only necessary kind of conferences—parent/child conferences are needed too. Are you interested in what your child does at school? Take him to a special place to talk about it. (Chuck E. Cheese might be too distracting!) Support him by asking questions—in a non-threatening way—such as if there are any areas at school in which he'd like to improve. Come up with solutions together and then have your child share his ideas with his teacher.

✔ Work

Employee evaluations are common in the workplace. Whether you work at home or in a large corporation, your work will be evaluated. How you receive this evaluation is critical to your success, and can make the difference between promotion and dismissal.

Show & Tell: Do you have periodic evaluations at work? Share the process with your child and let her know in what areas you are striving to improve. When your next evaluation takes place, update your child on your progress.

Family Activity

For school-age children one of the best ways for them to become a confident self-assessor is to evaluate their own schoolwork. This activity would ideally involve the entire family, but the child will receive the primary benefit.

The following activity will create a portfolio of learning for your child. You will need:

- a three-ring binder
- dividers
- your child's schoolwork.

Divide the three-ring binder into subject areas with the dividers. If you choose a binder with a front cover sleeve, have your child design a cover himself and then slip it into the front of the binder.

Each Friday go through any schoolwork your child brought home during that week and have him place it in the appropriate section of the notebook. Sorting through the papers provides a good opportunity to talk about the assignments and what your child learned. You could also help him think about how he might improve in a particular area.

Choose a time to have your child present his "portfolio of learning" to the other members of your family, as often as once a quarter or just at the end of the school year. Since the papers will be in a consecutive order, you and your child will be able to track his progress throughout the year.

When your child shares his portfolio, ensure that it is a safe environment, that he will be paid attention to and encouraged rather than teased or ignored. To make it a positive experience, you could go out to a favorite restaurant or even prepare a special dessert for that evening. If you are doing this with more than one child, let each have his own night to share.

When done on a regular basis, the practice of creating and sharing "portfolios of learning" accomplishes five things:

1. It shows your child that you value his education.
2. It shows your child that you are interested in how he is doing.
3. You become involved on a deeper level in your child's development day by day.
4. As your child is able to track his improvement, he will develop a sense of purpose and pride.
5. Your child can see his strengths and weaknesses, and it motivates him to improve.

A portfolio of learning is a valuable tool for developing confident self-assessors. And if you keep your children's portfolios from year to year, you will have a fun memento to look back on as they get older.

Coaching Your Child's Achievement

Remember: Your role is to be the *coach* of your child's achievement—not the taskmaster! If you did nothing specific to teach your child to apply these strategies, you could still raise a successful child simply by effectively modeling the strategies. Work on your *own* understanding and implementation of these strategies first: This is the most important part of teaching your child to apply them for himself.

Your family provides the best learning environment your child will ever have. You have a greater stake in your child's future than any school will, because you love your children more than any teacher could. Don't target too many areas of improvement in your child before you have dealt with them in yourself. Chances are, if your child lacks a specific skill or ability, *you do as well.* If you find this to be the case, tackle them one at a time and learn the new skill together. That will make it fun and inspiring.

As the ultimate coach of your child's success, you must provide not just rules to follow, but competencies to apply. Always lead with love, patience, and understanding, and always encourage your children to persevere. And remember: Just as a good coach models a skill by first showing the player how to do it, and then supervises the practice before the first game, you must model and supervise the development of life skills in your children. You are their life coach—and the game is the game of life.

Appendix

Parents' Multiple Intelligence Inventory

It has been suggested that there are at least seven different "types" of intelligence.[1] Depending on your background and age, you will have developed in more of these than others. This list should help you determine your strengths and weaknesses.

Check each statement that applies.

1. Linguistic Intelligence

____ Books are very important to me.

____ I can hear words in my head before I read, speak, or write them down.

____ I get more out of listening to the radio or a spoken word cassette than I do from television or films.

____ I enjoy word games like *Scrabble, Anagrams,* or *Password.*

____ I enjoy entertaining others or myself with tongue twisters, nonsense rhymes, or puns.

____ Other people sometimes have to stop and ask me to explain the meaning of the words I use in my writing and speaking.

____ English, social studies, and history were easier for me in school than math and science.

____ When I drive down a freeway, I pay more attention to the words written on billboards than I do to the scenery.

____ My conversation includes frequent references to things that I've read or heard.

____ I've written something recently that I was particularly proud of or that earned me recognition from others.

2. Logical/Mathematical Intelligence

____ I can easily compute numbers in my head.

____ Math and/or science were among my favorite subjects in school.

____ I enjoy playing games or solving brainteasers that require logical thinking.

____ I like to set up little "what-if" experiments. (For example, "What if I double the amount of water I give my rosebush each week?")

____ My mind searches for patterns, regularities, or logical sequences in things.

____ I believe that almost everything has a rational explanation.

____ I sometimes think in clear, abstract, wordless, imageless concepts.

____ I like finding logical flaws in things that people say and do at home and work.

____ I feel more comfortable when something has been measured, categorized, analyzed, or quantified in some way.

3. Spatial Intelligence

____ I often see clear visual images when I close my eyes.

____ I'm sensitive to color.

____ I frequently use a camera or camcorder to record what I see around me.

____ I enjoy doing jigsaw puzzles, mazes, and other visual puzzles.

____ I have vivid dreams at night.

____ I can generally find my way around unfamiliar territory.

____ I like to draw or doodle.

____ Geometry was easier for me than algebra in school.

____ I can comfortably imagine how something might appear if it were looked at from directly above (a bird's-eye view).

____ I prefer looking at reading material that is heavily illustrated.

4. Bodily/Kinesthetic Intelligence

____ I engage in at least one sport or physical activity on a regular basis.

____ I find it difficult to sit still for long periods of time.

____ I like working with my hands at concrete activities such as sewing, weaving, carving, carpentry, or building models.

____ My best ideas often come to me when I'm out for a long walk or a jog, or when I'm engaging in some other kind of physical activity.

____ I need to touch something in order to learn more about it.

____ I enjoy daredevil amusement rides or similar thrilling physical experiences.

____ I would describe myself as well coordinated.

____ I need to actively practice a new skill rather than simply reading about it or seeing a video that describes it.

5. Musical Intelligence

____ I have a pleasant singing voice.

____ I can tell when a musical note is off-key.

____ I frequently listen to music on radio, records, cassettes, or CDs.

____ I play a musical instrument.

____ My life would be poorer if there were no music in it.

____ I sometimes catch myself walking down the street with a television jingle or other tune running through my head.

____ I know the tunes to many different songs or musical pieces.

____ If I hear a musical selection once or twice, I am usually able to sing it back somewhat accurately.

____ I often make tapping sounds or sing melodies while working, studying, or learning something new.

6. Interpersonal Intelligence

____ I'm the sort of person that people come to for advice and counsel at work or in my community.

____ I prefer group sports such as badminton, volleyball, or softball to solo sports such as swimming or jogging.

____ When I have a problem, I'm more likely to seek out another person to help than attempt to work it out on my own.

____ I have at least three close friends.

____ I favor social pastimes such as playing *Monopoly* or bridge over individual recreations such as playing video games and solitaire.

____ I enjoy the challenge of teaching another person, or groups of people, what I know how to do.

____ I consider myself a leader (or others have called me that).

____ I feel comfortable in the midst of a crowd.

____ I like to be involved in social activities connected with my work, church, or community.

____ I would rather spend my evenings at a lively party than stay at home alone.

7. Intrapersonal Intelligence

____ I regularly spend time alone meditating, reflecting, or thinking about important life questions.

____ I have attended counseling sessions or personal growth seminars to learn more about myself.

____ I am able to respond to setbacks with resilience.

____ I have a special hobby or interest that keeps me pretty much to myself.

____ I have some important goals for my life that I think about on a regular basis.

____ I have a realistic view of my strengths and weaknesses (according to feedback from other sources).

____ I would prefer to spend a weekend alone in a cabin in the woods rather than at a fancy resort with lots of people around.

____ I consider myself to be strong-willed or independently minded.

____ I keep a personal diary or journal to record the events of my inner life.

____ I am self-employed or have at least thought seriously about starting my own business.

Total Score

____ **Linguistic**

____ **Logical/Mathematical**

____ **Spatial**

____ **Bodily/Kinesthetic**

____ **Musical**

____ **Interpersonal**

____ **Intrapersonal**

Child's Multiple Intelligence Inventory

Help your child check all that apply, then add up the check marks to rate his strength in that category.[2]

Verbal/Linguistic Intelligence

____ I enjoy telling stories and jokes.

____ I have a good memory for trivia.

____ I enjoy word games such as *Scrabble* and other puzzles.

____ I read books just for fun.

____ I am a good speller (most of the time).

____ In an argument I tend to use put-downs or sarcasm.

____ I like talking and writing about my ideas.

____ If I have to memorize something, I create a rhyme or saying to help me remember.

____ If something breaks and won't work, I read the instruction book.

____ For a group presentation I prefer to do the writing and library research.

Logical/Mathematical Intelligence

____ I really enjoy math class.

____ I like logical math puzzles or brainteasers.

____ I find solving math problems to be fun.

____ If I have to memorize something, I tend to place events in a logical order.

____ I like to find out how things work.

____ I enjoy computer and math games.

____ I love playing chess, checkers, or *Monopoly.*

____ In an argument, I try to find a fair and logical solution.

____ If something breaks and won't work, I look at the pieces and try to figure out how it works.

____ For a group presentation I prefer to create the charts and graphs.

Visual/Spatial Intelligence

____ I prefer a map to written directions.

____ I daydream a lot.

____ I enjoy hobbies such as photography.

____ I like to draw and create pictures.

____ If I have to memorize something, I draw a diagram to help me remember.

____ I like to doodle on paper whenever I can.

____ In a magazine, I prefer looking at the pictures to reading the text.

____ In an argument I try to keep my distance, keep silent, or try to visualize some solution.

____ If something breaks and won't work, I study the diagram of how it works.

____ For a group presentation I prefer to draw all the pictures.

Bodily/Kinesthetic Intelligence

____ My favorite class is gym since I like sports.

____ I enjoy activities such as woodworking, sewing, or building models.

____ When I look at things, I like to touch them.

____ I have trouble sitting still for any length of time.

____ I use a lot of body movements when talking.

____ If I have to memorize something, I write it out a number of times until I know it.

_____ I tend to tap my fingers or play with my pencil during class.

_____ In a argument I tend to strike out and hit or run away.

_____ If something breaks and won't work, I tend to play with the pieces to try to fit them together.

_____ For a group presentation I prefer to move the props around, hold things up, or build a model.

Musical/Rhythmic Intelligence

_____ I enjoy listening to CDs and the radio.

_____ I tend to hum to myself when working.

_____ I like to sing.

_____ I play a musical instrument quite well.

_____ I like to have music playing when I'm doing homework or studying.

_____ If I have to memorize something, I try to create a rhyme about the event.

_____ In an argument I tend to shout or punch or move in some sort of rhythm.

_____ I can remember the melodies of many songs.

_____ If something breaks and won't work, I tend to tap my fingers to a beat while I figure it out.

_____ For a group presentation I prefer to put new words to a popular tune or use music in any way possible.

Interpersonal Intelligence

_____ I get along well with others.

_____ I belong to several clubs and organizations.

_____ I have several very close friends.

_____ I like helping to teach other students.

_____ I like working with others in groups.

____ Friends ask my advice because I seem to be a natural leader.

____ If I have to memorize something, I ask someone else to quiz me to see if I know it.

____ In an argument I tend to ask a friend or some person in authority for help.

____ If something breaks and won't work, I try to find someone who can help me.

____ For a group presentation I like to help organize the group's efforts.

Intrapersonal Intelligence

____ I like to work alone without anyone else bothering me.

____ I like to keep a diary.

____ I like myself (most of the time).

____ I don't like crowds.

____ I know what I am good at and what I am weak at.

____ I am strong-willed, independent, and I don't usually follow the crowd.

____ If I have to memorize something, I tend to close my eyes and feel the situation.

____ In an argument I will usually walk away until I calm down.

____ If something breaks and won't work, I wonder if it's worth fixing.

____ For a group presentation I like to contribute something that is uniquely mine, often based on how I feel.

Naturalist Intelligence

____ I am keenly aware of my surroundings and of what goes on around me.

____ I love to walk in the woods and look at the trees and flowers.

____ I enjoy gardening.

____ I like to collect things such as rocks, sports cards, or stamps.

____ As an adult, I would like to live away from the city where I could enjoy nature.

____ If I have to memorize something, I tend to organize it into categories.

____ I enjoy learning the names of living things in our environment, such as flowers and trees.

____ In an argument I tend to compare my opponent to someone or something I have read or heard about and react accordingly.

____ If something breaks down, I look around me to try and see what I can find to fix the problem.

____ For a group presentation I prefer to organize and classify the information into categories so it makes sense.

Total Score

____ **Verbal/Linguistic**

____ **Logical/Mathematical**

____ **Visual/Spatial**

____ **Bodily/Kinesthetic**

____ **Musical/Rhythmic**

____ **Interpersonal**

____ **Intrapersonal**

____ **Naturalist**

Notes

Introduction

1. *"What Work Requires of Schools,"* SCANS report, National Technical Information Service (NTIS), Technology Administration, U.S. Department of Commerce, Springfield, Va., 1991.

Chapter One

1. According to Dr. Brian Ray, president of the National Home Education Research Institute, there were approximately 1.5 to 1.9 million children (grades K-12) home-educated in the United States during the 2000-2001 school year.

2. For more information on homeschooling, see Vicki's books, *The ABCs of Homeschooling* (Wheaton, Ill.: Crossway Books, 2001) and *The Organized Homeschooler* (Wheaton, Ill.: Crossway Books, 2001).

3. Schools and Staffing Survey, U.S. Department of Education, 1995.

Chapter Three

1. Linda Kavelin Popov, *The Family Virtues Guide* (New York: Plume, 1997), 105.

2. Ibid., 225.

Chapter Four

1. Quoted in *Teaching Creative Behavior,* Shallcross Doris (New York: Bearly Limited, 1985), foreword.

2. Popov, *The Family Virtues Guide*, 98.

3. Eugene Raudsepp, *How Creative Are You?* (New York: Perigree, 1981), 105.

4. Ibid.

5. Taken from www.creativelearning.com, D.J. Treffinger.

6. D. J. Treffinger, *Practice Problems for Creative Problem Solving* (Waco, Texas: Prufrock Press, 2000). Reprinted with permission.

Chapter Five

1. All references to the "Webster's Dictionary" are taken from *Merriam—Webster's Collegiate® Dictionary*, 10th edition (Mass.: Merriam-Webster, Inc., 2000).

2. Vincent Ruggerio, *The Art of Thinking*, 3rd edition (New York: HarperCollins, 1987), 180-184.

3. Jessie Wise and Susan Wise Bauer, *The Well-Trained Mind* (New York: W. W. Norton & Co., 1999), 242.

4. The Great Books Foundation Web site lists these and other helpful ideas (www.greatbooks.org).

Chapter Six

1. For more advanced learners *The Elements of Style* by Strunk and White (New York: Macmillan, 1999) and *The Chicago Manual of Style* (Chicago: University of Chicago Press, 1993) show how to cite various sources of information for bibliographies.

2. Robert I. Fitzhenry, *The Harper Book of Quotations*, 3rd edition (New York: HarperPerennial, 1993), 327.

Chapter Seven

1. Popov, *The Family Virtues Guide*, 69.

2. Ibid., 201.

3. Ibid., 78.

4. Adapted from *Social Skills Activities for Special Children* by Darlene Mannix (New York: The Center for Applied Research in Education, 1993), 2.

Chapter Eight

1. William Strunk, Jr. and E. B. White, *The Elements of Style*, 3rd edition (Needham Heights, Mass.: Allyn & Bacon, 1979), 23.

2. Ruggerio, *The Art of Thinking,* 218.

3. Ruggerio, 221.

4. Adapted from the "Socratic Questioning Techniques" Web site (www.covington.k12.tn.us/resources/question.htm), (accessed July 13, 2003).

5. Nathan Levy's books are available from NL Associates, Inc., P.O. Box 1199, Hightstown, NJ 08520.

Chapter Nine

1. John Maxwell, *The 21 Indispensable Qualities of a Leader* (Nashville: Thomas Nelson, 1999), introduction.

2. Ibid., 77.

3. Ibid., 107.

4. Eugene B. Habecker, *The Other Side of Leadership,* (Wheaton, Ill.: Victor Books, 1987).

5. See *The Five Love Languages* by Gary Chapman (Chicago: Northfield Publishing, 1992).

Chapter Ten

1. Available at the Henry J. Kaiser Family Foundation Web site: www.kff.org.

2. Tom Loveless, "School Success Begins at Home," USA Weekend, August 26, 2001.
3. Ibid.
4. See www.bgca.org.

Chapter Eleven

1. Robert Merton, *Social Theory and Social Structure* (New York: The Free Press, 1968), referenced in "Self-fulfilling Prophecy or Pygmalion Effect," Accel Team Web site, accessed August 22, 2003 (www.accel-team.com/pygmalion/).

Appendix

1. Adapted from the book *7 Kinds of Smart* by Thomas Armstrong (New York: Plume Books, 1993).
2. From *Multiple Intelligences,* 2nd edition by Thomas Armstrong (Alexandria, Va.: Association for Supervision and Curriculum Development, 2000). Reprinted by permission. All rights reserved.

FOCUS ON THE FAMILY®

Welcome to the *Family!*

Whether you received this book as a gift, borrowed it, or purchased it yourself, we're glad you read it. It's just one of the many helpful, insightful, and encouraging resources produced by Focus on the Family.

In fact, that's what Focus on the Family is all about—providing inspiration, information, and biblically based advice to people in all stages of life.

It began in 1977 with the vision of one man, Dr. James Dobson, a licensed psychologist and author of 18 best-selling books on marriage, parenting, and family. Alarmed by the societal, political, and economic pressures that were threatening the existence of the American family, Dr. Dobson founded Focus on the Family with one employee and a once-a-week radio broadcast aired on only 36 stations.

Now an international organization, the ministry is dedicated to preserving Judeo-Christian values and strengthening and encouraging families through the life-changing message of Jesus Christ. Focus ministries reach families worldwide through 10 separate radio broadcasts, two television news features, 13 publications, 18 Web sites, and a steady series of books and award-winning films and videos for people of all ages and interests.

•   •   •

For more information about the ministry, or if we can be of help to your family, simply write to Focus on the Family, Colorado Springs, CO 80995 or call (800) A-FAMILY (232-6459). Friends in Canada may write Focus on the Family, P.O. Box 9800, Stn. Terminal, Vancouver, B.C .V6B 4G3 or call (800) 661-9800. Visit our Web site—www.family.org—to learn more about Focus on the Family or to find out if there is an associate office in your country.

We'd love to hear from you!

Parenting Solutions
From Focus on the Family®

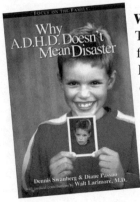

Why A.D.H.D. Doesn't Mean Disaster
This book provides a realistic, encouraging perspective from parents who have raised children with ADHD. Filled with insights, personal stories and sound medical expertise, parents facing the challenges of handling ADHD will find hope that breaks through the hype. Hardcover.

The Way They Learn
Learning styles expert Cynthia Tobias gives parents a better understanding of the learning approaches that will help their children do better in school. Once these approaches are understood, any parent or teacher can become effective in helping any child grasp confusing concepts, stay interested in lessons and utilize his or her greatest strengths. Paperback.

Your Child Membership Program
This membership offers parents with children 12 and under age-customized parenting tips, fun activities and more through newsletters, audio journals and Web site features. Visit us at www.focusonyourchild.com and sign up for your complimentary membership. (Available in the U.S. only.)

Look for these special resources in your Christian bookstore or request an item by calling (800) A-FAMILY (232-6459). Friends in Canada may write to Focus on the Family, P.O. Box 9800, Stn. Terminal, Vancouver, B.C. V6B 4G3 or call (800) 661-9800.

Visit our Web site (www.family.org) to learn more about the ministry or to find out if there is a Focus on the Family office in your country.

Vicki Caruana is foremost a teacher, speaking at educational and homeschooling conferences nationwide. She is a frequent guest on various radio and television broadcasts and her writing appears in many magazines. She is the founder of *Teachers in Prayer*. Vicki lives in Colorado Springs, Colorado.

To contact the author:
Vicki Caruana
P.O. Box 9231
Colorado Springs, CO 80909
www.applesandchalkdust.com
vcaruana@aol.com

To schedule a speaking engagement, contact Speak Up Speaker Services at www.speakupspeakerservices.com